Taming the
Data Monster

Taming the Data Monster

Collecting and Analyzing Classroom Data to Improve Student Progress

Christine Reeve, PhD, BCBA-D
Susan Kabot, EdD, CCC-SLP

Foreword by Jim Ball, EdD, BCBA-D

11209 Strang Line Rd
Lenexa, KS 66215
www.aapcpublishing.net

© 2016 AAPC
11209 Strang Line Rd
Lenexa, KS 66215
www.aapcpublishing.net

Publisher's Cataloging-in-Publication

Reeve, Christine E.

Taming the data monster : collecting and analyzing classroom data to improve
student progress / Christine Reeve, Susan Kabot. -- First edition.
-- Shawnee Mission, KS : AAPC Publishing, [2016]

pages ; cm.

ISBN: 978-1-942197-07-2
LCCN: 2015944904
Includes bibliographical references.
Summary: Faced with increasing demands for accountability, teachers are having to base their instructional decisions and choice of interventions on data on student performance. This book shows how to make this otherwise daunting task much more manageable by means of case studies and countless evidence-based forms and graphs. Blank forms are available online.--Publisher.

    1. Teachers of children with disabilities--Statistical methods--Study and teaching. 2. Autistic children--Education--Statistical methods--Study and teaching. 3. Children with autism spectrum disorders--Education--Statistical methods--Study and teaching. 4. Autism spectrum disorders--Patients--Education--Statistical methods--Study and teaching. 5. Education research--Study and teaching. 6. Educational statistics--Study and teaching. 7. Educational tests and measurements--Study and teaching. 8. Multivariate analysis--Study and teaching. 9. Data mining--Study and teaching. I. Kabot, Susan. II. Title.

LC4717.8 .R448 2015
371.94--dc23   1508

This book is designed in Adobe Garamond, Minion and Trebuchet
Printed in the United States of America

Contents

Foreword

Data collection and analysis are some of the most important tools professionals have to determine and subsequently improve student performance, be it academic or behavioral. Unfortunately, this topic is probably the least trained and most misunderstood. We tend to take data because someone told us to do it, spending a great deal of time investigating the function of behavior and designing programs without giving careful attention to choosing the most effective and easy-to-use data collection system.

Data-based decision making is one of the most important aspects of successful student programming, but choosing a data collection system can be difficult. There are many ways to collect data, and picking the best system can mean the difference between success and failure. *Taming the Data Monster: Collecting and Analyzing Classroom Data to Improve Student Progress* allows readers to look at the different systems and assists them in choosing the system that is most appropriate for their program and students.

Data collection can be cumbersome and overwhelming and is often perceived as boring and unnecessary. This is where *Taming the Data Monster: Collecting and Analyzing Classroom Data to Improve Student Progress* is valuable as it presents an abundance of ready-made data sheets that can be used to track skills and behaviors. The best feature of this book is the section on analyzing the data once it has been recorded. It walks the reader through how to graph data and then how to read it and make good decisions. What I love the most about this book is that as you read through it and become comfortable with the content, data collection becomes easier and easier!

In short, *Taming the Data Monster: Collecting and Analyzing Classroom Data to Improve Student Progress* explains in a very concise way the best options for collecting and analyzing data. It takes the guesswork out and assists with the development of effective data collection systems that are easy to analyze. This book is a necessary addition to the library of any professional who works with students with special needs.

Jim Ball, EdD, BCBA-D

Chapter 1
Introduction

In our practice of providing training and consultation to school districts throughout the country, as well as in programs for students with autism spectrum disorder (ASD) that we have administered, the design and implementation of data collection protocols for both skill acquisition and behavior reduction have presented us with our greatest challenges. We have heard all of the reasons people give for why data collection can't be performed, including the great amount of time it takes, interference with actual teaching, paraprofessionals who can't be trained to do it, data collection methods being too complicated … and why it is not necessary: "I'm keeping the information in my head."

Although this book often refers to students and classrooms, the data collection techniques are applicable to a wide range of environments, including clinics, job-training and actual job sites, and homes. In addition, the data collection tools and procedures are relevant for use with a wide range of ages, from toddlers to adults.

With many years of experience trying out data collection techniques and forms ourselves, training school-based staff to collect and analyze data, and listening to feedback from staff at many levels, we have developed or selected data sheets and designed data collection systems that are easy to use during the regular course of the staff's activities. Of course, the collection of data is only the first step in understanding the student's progress in acquiring skills and/or improving behavior. Often, analysis of the data presents greater barriers than the actual collection of the data, with binders of completed data sheets often ending up unused on classroom shelves.

If the staff responsible for monitoring an individual's progress is not able to quickly and easily see how the person is progressing towards behavioral targets or academic goals and objectives, then the collection of data is not serving the purpose it was intended to meet. Analyzing trends in the data is critical for revising instructional programs and behavior intervention plans.

We hope that you will find this book to be a useful resource as you work to improve outcomes for individuals with ASD and other significant disabilities.

What Is "Data"?

Data can be defined as a method of quantifying student outcomes in relation to curriculum and individually developed goals and objectives for learning and behavior. It serves as a method of substantiating student performance against established criteria or norms. In addition, data provides information for making adjustments to teaching strategies or behavior reduction programs based on the student's performance.

The Importance of Data Collection and Analysis

From early childhood through adulthood, data is being collected at various levels within all types of support systems. Caregivers and instructors across a variety of settings are increasingly being asked to collect data to document progress in the acquisition of learning and behavior change for Individual Family Support Plans (IFSP), Individual Educational Programs (IEP), Individual Habilitation Plans (IHP), functional behavior assessments (FBA), and behavior support plans to prevent and reduce challenging behavior. However, collecting data is not sufficient. The data needs to be analyzed. We must use the data to make decisions about the effectiveness of our instruction and behavior change processes. Research has shown that student performance improves when teachers collect data on a regular basis and analyze the data to make instructional decisions (Browder, Liberty, Heller, & D'Huyvetterf, 1986; Farlow & Snell, 1984; Jimenez, Mims, & Browder, 2012).

TABLE 1.1

Reasons for Collecting and Analyzing Data

Reasons for Collecting and Analyzing Data

- To provide an objective and reliable method of assessing change in learning and behavior.
- To document progress against standards, norms, or curricula (Common Core, State Standards, developmental milestones).
- To improve the efficiency and effectiveness of instruction and behavior change programs for students.
- To assess and document progress in skill acquisition and challenging behavior reduction.
- To provide legal accountability for mandated programs (e.g., IEP, Response to Intervention [RTI]).
- To provide information for resolving difficulties in making progress.
- To provide a common language for regular and meaningful communication of a student's progress to relevant parties (e.g., parents, state agencies).
- To document implementation of specific interventions and strategies.

Meet the Teachers

Throughout the book, we will illustrate various data collection and analysis procedures, including methods to help organize the collection of data within different environments using the following instructors as case studies.

SALLY. Our first case is Sally, an elementary school teacher who has just started working with students with ASD and related disabilities in a special education classroom. A second-year teacher, Sally feels that she has the classroom well organized but finds that she is struggling with how to take data on her students and use it in a meaningful way. The parents of the students in her classroom, as well as her administrators, keep telling her how important data are and that they want to review the data to talk about the students' progress, but Sally isn't sure how to add this to the already daunting task of planning for and keeping students engaged in instruction.

Sally has tried various methods of taking data, each time thinking she has found a solution, only to find that she ends up with lots of papers that pile up and do nothing to help her instruction. When administrators or parents ask to see the data, Sally isn't sure what to show them and finds herself staying up half the night before IEP meetings trying to gather and make sense of the information she has. Sally struggled last year with data and had difficulty managing the forms while trying to work with the students. She usually ended up relying on remembering what happened at the end of the day but realized that was not a good solution because many times she lost track of the students' performance over the six-hour day.

Recently, a new autism consultant in the district, Myra, met with Sally to identify the areas where Sally felt she needed assistance. One of the areas Sally wanted to work on was the development of usable data collection systems, with easy methods to analyze and use data to make decisions about the students' progress and make changes to instruction. The following figures show the types of strategies that Myra and Sally developed to help tame the data monster. Each of these strategies will be addressed in more depth in the book. (A full description of the solutions for Sally is presented in Chapter 8.)

Comprehensive Autism Planning System (CAPS)/Teaching Plan

Student:	Common Reinforcers *(embedded throughout the day)*
Communication System:	Sensory Strategies *(embedded throughout the day)*
Date Completed:	Case Manager / Teacher:
Grade:	School Year:

For students served primarily in self-contained classrooms or as part of the process for designing a self-contained classroom, begin completing the following grid with the student's IEP and curriculum objectives to build the schedule. For students who are primarily participating in a general education classroom, you might start with the schedule column and target the goals/skills from that, completing the rest of the grid as needed.

Goal/Objective/ Targeted Skill	Primary Teaching Activity/ Scheduled Activity	Teaching Strategy	Structure/ Modifications/ Accommodations	Reinforcers	Communication/ Social Supports	Data Collection	Generalization Plan

Created by Reeve and Kabot. Modified from Henry, S.A., & Myles, B.S. (2013). *The Comprehensive Autism Planning System (CAPS) for individuals with autism spectrum and related disabilities: Integrating evidence-based practices throughout the student's day* (2nd ed.). Shawnee Mission, KS: AAPC Publishing.

Figure 1.1. The Comprehesive Autism Planning System (CAPS).
The CAPS allows Sally to outline where and when data collection will occur in the daily routine and the format the data collection will take.

Sally's Zoning Plan (Excerpt)

Time/Activity	Sally	Chrissy	Robert	Comments
7:30-8:15 Arrival/Breakfast	Start at cafeteria; bring back N and S, bathroom students as you are able	Start at cafeteria, remain in cafeteria until all students have arrived; then escort students to room	Start at cafeteria, remain in cafeteria until all students or most of students have arrived, then escort to class	
8:15-8:30 Table Tasks	Transition first students back to schedule and table tasks; man table tasks; take data on two students' targeted goals each day	Transition students back to classroom, check their schedule, and check into table tasks; begin to pull students for bathroom one to two at a time; toileting data for B and S	Transition students back to classroom, check their schedule, and check into table tasks; begin to pull students for bathroom one to two at a time; toileting data for B and S	
8:30-8:45 Journals	Supervise journals, help students complete their page and tell about it if they can	Continue to pull students to bathroom and assist with journals when available	Continue to pull students to bathroom and assist with journals when available	Work product data collection
8:45-9:00 Circle	Run circle	Prompt and assist all students, particularly S; take data on one designated student's targeted goals/day	Prompt and assist all students, particularly N; take data on one designated student's targeted goals/day	
9:00-9:15 Centers 1	Reading with C and S; take daily data	Individual work with B and A; take data on one student per day	Art with N and N; take data on one student per day	
9:15-9:30 Centers 2	Reading with N and N; take daily data	IW with C and S; take data on one student per day	Art with B and A; take data on one student per day	
9:30-9:45 Centers 3	Reading with B and A; take daily data	IW with N and N; set up table tasks; take data on one student per day	Art with C and S; take data on one student per day	Mon and Thurs C goes to speech
9:45-10:00 TT/BR	Pull students 1-2 at a time for bathroom; toileting data for B and S	Pull students 1-2 at a time for bathroom; toileting data for B and S	Supervise table tasks	
10:00-10:30 PE/Gym	Stay to make sure choice time is ready, then join PE	Accompany students to PE; take data on one student per day	Accompany students to PE; take data on one student per day	

Figure 1.2. Sally's zoning plan for her classroom.
The plan outlines the staff's responsibilities across the day. The highlighted items indicate when they are collecting data.

DISCRETE TRIAL DATA COLLECTION FORM

SKILL:	MONTH:	YEAR:	CHILD'S NAME:
Primary Instructor:	Target Behavior: Student will identify correct letter when told the sound it makes		
S^d: "What letter makes the _____ sound?"	Prerequisites for Skill:		

PROCEDURAL STEPS		
1. Correctly identifies cards of letters making first sound. 2. Correctly identifies cards of letter making second sound. 3. Randomly identifies cards of letters making learned sounds. Repeat steps 1-3 for two new concepts.	Have student choose the letters from written letters in an array of 5	

DATE:																		
STEP:																		
Graph of Progress: Circle percentage of mastery for Each session; If it is uneven (e.g., 30%) place an X between the printed percentages	100	100	100	100	100	100	100	100	100	100	100	100	100	100	100	100	100	100
	80	80	80	80	80	80	80	80	80	80	80	80	80	80	80	80	80	80
	60	60	60	60	60	60	60	60	60	60	60	60	60	60	60	60	60	60
	40	40	40	40	40	40	40	40	40	40	40	40	40	40	40	40	40	40
	20	20	20	20	20	20	20	20	20	20	20	20	20	20	20	20	20	20
	0	0	0	0	0	0	0	0	0	0	0	0	0	0	0	0	0	0
Trial 1																		
Trial 2																		
Trial 3																		
Trial 4																		
Trial 5																		
STAFF INITIALS:																		

Scoring Code	Lower Triangle Code	Reinforcers	Comments/Observations:
+-Independent x-Incorrect I-Visual G-Gestural O-Positional V-Verbal P-Physical	Write in the letter corresponding to the body part letter being taught in that trial	Reinforcer Schedule ☐ Fixed Ratio 1:1 ☐ Fixed Ratio 2:1 ☐ Variable Ratio	___/___/_____ ___/___/_____ ___/___/_____ ___/___/_____ ___/___/_____ ___/___/_____

Adapted from Nova Southeastern University Autism Program. Used with permission.

Figure 1.3. Discrete trial data sheet.
The data sheet self-graphs. It will be discussed with examples later in the book. It is used during 1-1 or small-group instruction.

Figure 1.4. Organization tools.
Sally uses drawers in carts to organize her data collection forms and teaching materials.

Naturalistic Sample Data Sheet

Activity: Morning Meeting		Teacher: Sally McKenzie		Week: 9/26/16
Sydney	**Calen**	**Noni**	**Bill**	**Naomi**
Follows teacher directions to the group	Respond to greetings from adults	Recognizes her name by selecting it from field of 2	Recognizes picture by selecting from field 2	Recognizes picture by selecting from field 2
Answers "What is it?" with a sentence	Requests a break	Follows a 1-step direction	Responds to greeting from adult with gesture /vocalization	Follows a 1-step direction
Identifies classmates by pointing or using their name	Identifies classmates by pointing or using their name	Requests a break	Responds to greeting from adult with gesture /vocalization	Follows a 1-step direction
Responds to greeting from adult verbally	Follows directions given to the group	Answers a question in 2-3 word sentence	Identifies classmates by pointing or using their name	Identifies classmates by pointing or using their name

+ = Independent P = Prompted X = Incorrect 0 = No Response

Figure 1.5. Naturalistic sample data sheet.

Sally can use a naturalistic sample data sheet for a group to collect data samples on multiple students within a group activity throughout the week. The data sheet also serves to remind the staff what goals are being targeted.

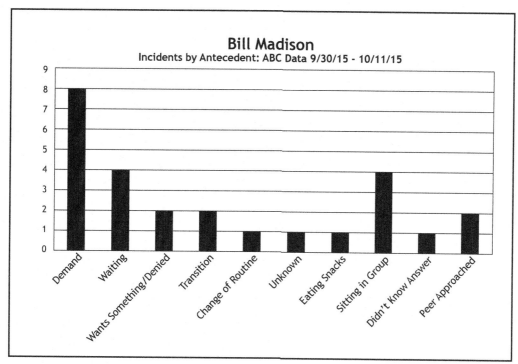

Figure 1.6. Data on Bill's behavior.
Sally collected data on Bill's behavior as part of a functional behavior assessment. She then graphed the data of challenging behavior by common antecedents to try to determine the function of a given behavior.

SAM. Sam is a general education high school teacher who suddenly has four students with special needs in his classroom. Sam has participated in the students' IEP meetings and knows that tracking students' progress is something the educational team thinks is important and required by law. However, he is used to applying grades on assignments as his data tracking system, along with scores on standardized tests, and he feels very unprepared to monitor behavior and social skills goals that have been identified for the students in his class. He has had students with special needs in his classes before and is comfortable with their accommodations and modifications, but this is the first time he has students who have goals in behavior and social skills that need to be tracked.

Each student has an assigned special education case manager, but the case mangers are limited in how much time they can spend in the classroom because their caseload takes them all over the building. Consequently, Sam has to track these skills in some manner on his own. What makes this especially challenging is that he won't have a paraprofessional working in his classroom to help him like he has had before.

Sam is very concerned about the new school year because he sees himself spending a lot of time doing paperwork and, therefore, having less time to teach all of the students in his classes. Myra, the ASD consultant, has promised to help him develop some systems with the team to make tracking these skills easier and functional rather than simply forms that have to be completed every day. To tame the data monster for Sam, they put in place the strategies below, which will be discussed later in the book. (The full explanation of strategies implemented in Sam's classroom may be found in Chapter 8.)

Comprehensive Autism Planning System (CAPS)

Student: _____

Time	Activity	Targeted Skills to Teach	Structure/ Modifications	Reinforcement	Sensory Strategies	Communication/ Social Skills	Data Collection	Generalization Plan

Modified from Henry, S.A., & Myles, B.S. (2013). *The Comprehensive Autism Planning System (CAPS) for individuals with autism spectrum and related disabilities: Integrating evidence-based practices throughout the student's day* (2nd ed.). Shawnee Mission, KS: AAPC Publishing.

Figure 1.7. CAPS.
Sam's CAPS is set up by his schedule during the day with the targeted skills. The skills are those on the student's IEP.

Academic Travel Card

Name: _Sarah_____   Week: _____

Directions: Check off each item that applies to your period and give the card back to the student to return to: _____

	1st period	2nd period	3rd period	4th period	6th period	7th period
Monday	☐ Turn in homework ☐ Materials ready ☐ Took notes ☐ Participated	☐ Turn in homework ☐ Materials ready ☐ Took notes ☐ Participated	☐ Turn in homework ☐ Materials ready ☐ Took notes ☐ Participated	☐ Turn in homework ☐ Materials ready ☐ Took notes ☐ Participated	☐ Turn in homework ☐ Materials ready ☐ Took notes ☐ Participated	☐ Turn in homework ☐ Materials ready ☐ Took notes ☐ Participated
Tuesday	☐ Turn in homework ☐ Materials ready ☐ Took notes ☐ Participated	☐ Turn in homework ☐ Materials ready ☐ Took notes ☐ Participated	☐ Turn in homework ☐ Materials ready ☐ Took notes ☐ Participated	☐ Turn in homework ☐ Materials ready ☐ Took notes ☐ Participated	☐ Turn in homework ☐ Materials ready ☐ Took notes ☐ Participated	☐ Turn in homework ☐ Materials ready ☐ Took notes ☐ Participated
Wednesday	☐ Turn in homework ☐ Materials ready ☐ Took notes ☐ Participated	☐ Turn in homework ☐ Materials ready ☐ Took notes ☐ Participated	☐ Turn in homework ☐ Materials ready ☐ Took notes ☐ Participated	☐ Turn in homework ☐ Materials ready ☐ Took notes ☐ Participated	☐ Turn in homework ☐ Materials ready ☐ Took notes ☐ Participated	☐ Turn in homework ☐ Materials ready ☐ Took notes ☐ Participated
Thursday	☐ Turn in homework ☐ Materials ready ☐ Took notes ☐ Participated	☐ Turn in homework ☐ Materials ready ☐ Took notes ☐ Participated	☐ Turn in homework ☐ Materials ready ☐ Took notes ☐ Participated	☐ Turn in homework ☐ Materials ready ☐ Took notes ☐ Participated	☐ Turn in homework ☐ Materials ready ☐ Took notes ☐ Participated	☐ Turn in homework ☐ Materials ready ☐ Took notes ☐ Participated
Friday	☐ Turn in homework ☐ Materials ready ☐ Took notes ☐ Participated	☐ Turn in homework ☐ Materials ready ☐ Took notes ☐ Participated	☐ Turn in homework ☐ Materials ready ☐ Took notes ☐ Participated	☐ Turn in homework ☐ Materials ready ☐ Took notes ☐ Participated	☐ Turn in homework ☐ Materials ready ☐ Took notes ☐ Participated	☐ Turn in homework ☐ Materials ready ☐ Took notes ☐ Participated
Totals						
Comments						

If this is found, please return to: _____

Figure 1.8. Travel card.

The travel card (originally created by Laura Carpenter) moves with Sarah throughout the day. Sarah is responsible for carrying it and having each teacher check off the boxes that applied to her performance during a given class period. At the end of the day, she turns it in to Sam for safe keeping.

Work Sample Data Collection

Setting: (circle 1)   Sp.Ed.   Gen. Ed.   Speech   OT

Other_____

____ Independent (nothing else should be checked)
____ Physical proximity of adult ONLY
____ Prompting for initial performance ONLY

PROMPTING (Check all that apply)

Visual	_____	Gestural	_____
Model	_____	Verbal	_____
Physical	_____	Notes:	_____

Date: _____   Staff Initials: _____

Figure 1.9. Label.

Sam uses this label to record information on students' work product in the classroom and places it on the back of the completed assignment.

Weekly Data Checklist

Name:	Date:
Data Collector:	Teacher:

Initiating and Responding to Peer

Check all that apply: I – Independent P – Prompted	I / P (circle)	No Response	Inappropriate Response	Comments
1. Initiate interaction with peer (e.g., says hi)	I / P			
2. Respond to 1st peer statement	I / P			
3. Respond to 2nd peer statement	I / P			
4. Respond to 3rd peer statement	I / P			

Check all that apply: I – Independent P – Prompted	I / P (circle)	No Response	Inappropriate Response	Comments
1. Initiate interaction with peer (e.g., says hi)	I / P			
2. Respond to 1st peer statement	I / P			
3. Respond to 2nd peer statement	I / P			
4. Respond to 3rd peer statement	I / P			

Independence Goal

Walking in Hallway	Number of redirections	Comments
1. Social studies or science: Walked in hallway without aide, count number of redirections		
2. Speech: Walked in hallway without aide, count number of redirections		

Locating Materials	Did it independently	Number of redirections needed	Comments
1. Located correct materials on list			
2. Turned to correct section in binder			

Figure 1.10. Weekly data checklist.

This data checklist allows Sam to take a weekly sample of an individual student's social and independent skills.

Social Skills - Pragmatics
How Did I Do Today?

Name:	Date:
Activity:	Time:
Rater:	

For each skill, rate the student's behavior in the Score column with a 1, 2 or 3.

Skill	1	2	3	Score
Visually checks in with partner	Makes eye contact when listening to partner	Makes minimal eye contact when speaking to partner	Makes appropriate eye contact when speaking to partner	
Stands at least 12-18 inches from partner	Stands 6 inches from partner	Stands 12 inches from partner	Stands 18 inches from partner	
Matches facial expression to verbal message	Makes stated emotion on face in isolation	Has appropriate emotion on face in interaction 50% of time	Has appropriate emotion on face in interaction 80% of time	
Shifts gaze to what partner is looking at or listening to	Shifts gaze to what partner is looking at/listening to in fleeting manner	Shifts gaze to what partner is looking at/listening to	Shifts gaze to what partner is looking at/listening to and rechecks with partner	
Self-monitors when vocal volume is too loud	Identifies when vocal volume is too loud for situation 50% of time	Identifies when vocal volume is too loud 90% of time	Regulates vocal volume when he sees he's too loud without adult prompt	

COMMENTS:

Figure 1.11. Rubric.
Sam can use a rubric to evaluate social skills and other qualitative skills for a student on a weekly basis.

A-B-C Form (RTI Version)

NAME:	Observer:		Target Behavior:		
DATE	ACTIVITY (Fill in with activities specific to student)	What was happening before or while the behavior occurred? (Check all that apply)	BEHAVIOR (Check all that apply)	What happened after the behavior? (Check all that apply)	Comments
	☐ Bathroom ☐ Outside ☐ Homeroom ☐ Hallway ☐ Lunchroom ☐ ___ ☐ ___ ☐ ___	☐ Asked to work ☐ Given a direction ☐ Walking in hallway ☐ Waiting ☐ Working on task ☐ Assigned to work with a group ☐ Between activities ☐ A peer approached student to interact ☐ Change in routine ☐ Corrected ☐ Entered classroom ☐ Other ___	☐ Insulted peer ☐ Didn't follow teacher's direction ☐ Verbally told teacher "no" in response to direction ☐ Did not complete assigned task ☐ Got out the wrong materials ☐ Talked to peer (when not supposed to) ☐ Yelled in class ☐ Refuses to participate in group activity ☐ Participates in preferred activity ☐ Interferes with other students' activities ☐ Does not stop something when directed to by teacher ☐ Other ___	☐ Verbally redirected ☐ Verbally corrected ☐ Physically redirected ☐ Other student yelled/reprimanded her ☐ Other student interacted in some way ☐ Removed from setting ☐ Work demand adjusted ☐ Work demand withdrawn ☐ Redirected for a break ☐ Redirected to another activity/action ☐ New choices issued ☐ Other (Describe)	
	☐ Bathroom ☐ Outside ☐ Homeroom ☐ Hallway ☐ Lunchroom ☐ ___ ☐ ___ ☐ ___	☐ Asked to work ☐ Given a direction ☐ Walking in hallway ☐ Waiting ☐ Working on task ☐ Assigned to work with a group ☐ Between activities ☐ A peer approached student to interact ☐ Change in routine ☐ Corrected ☐ Entered classroom ☐ Other ___	☐ Insulted peer ☐ Didn't follow teacher's direction ☐ Verbally told teacher "no" in response to direction ☐ Did not complete assigned task ☐ Got out the wrong materials ☐ Talked to peer (when not supposed to) ☐ Yelled in class ☐ Refuses to participate in group activity ☐ Participates in preferred activity ☐ Interferes with other students' activities ☐ Does not stop something when directed to by teacher ☐ Other ___	☐ Verbally redirected ☐ Verbally corrected ☐ Physically redirected ☐ Other student yelled/reprimanded ☐ Other student interacted in some way ☐ Removed from setting ☐ Work demand adjusted ☐ Work demand withdrawn ☐ Redirected for a break ☐ Redirected to another activity/action ☐ New choices issued ☐ Other (Describe)	
	☐ Bathroom ☐ Outside ☐ Homeroom ☐ Hallway ☐ Lunchroom ☐ ___ ☐ ___ ☐ ___	☐ Asked to work ☐ Given a direction ☐ Walking in hallway ☐ Waiting ☐ Working on task ☐ Assigned to work with a group ☐ Between activities ☐ A peer approached student to interact ☐ Change in routine ☐ Corrected ☐ Entered classroom ☐ Other ___	☐ Insulted peer ☐ Didn't follow teacher's direction ☐ Verbally told teacher "no" in response to direction ☐ Did not complete assigned task ☐ Got out the wrong materials ☐ Talked to peer (when not supposed to) ☐ Yelled in class ☐ Refuses to participate in group activity ☐ Participates in preferred activity ☐ Interferes with other students' activities ☐ Does not stop something when directed to by teacher ☐ Other ___	☐ Verbally redirected ☐ Verbally corrected ☐ Physically redirected ☐ Other student yelled/reprimanded ☐ Other student interacted in some way ☐ Removed from setting ☐ Work demand adjusted ☐ Work demand withdrawn ☐ Redirected for a break ☐ Redirected to another activity/action ☐ New choices issued ☐ Other (Describe)	

Figure 1.12. A-B-C form.

To reduce the amount of time required to take data for a functional behavior assessment in the general education classroom, Sam can use an ABC checklist to check off antecedents, behavior, and consequences as they occur.

JENNY. Jenny teaches a high school class for eight students with a variety of disabilities. She and her students spend one half to three quarters of their time in the community on job sites and completing independent living activities. Consequently, many of their goals and objectives for instruction involve performance on sites outside of the school.

Jenny has been teaching for 20 years and has had no difficulty recruiting community job opportunities for her students, setting up job sites, and providing the visual supports to help her students be as independent as possible. However, throughout the years she has struggled with how to manage data collection to track her students' skills while in the community. She has tried a variety of methods of data collection, including:

- An individual data sheet for each skill for each student.
- A data sheet for all the students with all their objectives that ended up being four pages long.
- Checklists for the task analyses for the skills each student was working on in notebooks for each student.
- Videotaping the students performing their jobs at selected times.

All of these systems have worked to some degree, but Jenny still finds that she often doesn't have the information she needs readily available when she needs it. For instance, while the videotaping worked to show the students' performance, it didn't capture the performance of each student across different placements. In order to get something she could use to monitor progress quantitatively, she had to go back and watch the videos and take data on them at a later time. This ended up being very time consuming.

Jenny has asked Myra to help her to develop a data collection system that is portable, easy to use in the community, and that allows her to track progress in a timely and consistent manner as efficiently as possible. She also asked for help with assigning who will be taking the data and training the paraprofessionals and job coaches who support the students in the community in data collection. She has found that sometimes each person thinks another is supposed to be taking the data, and, consequently, the information does not get recorded. She is looking for a way to address this issue.

To help Jenny develop and implement a manageable data collection system out in the community, Myra and Jenny chose the following strategies. These strategies will be discussed throughout the book. (A summary of the solutions for Jenny's classroom may be found in Chapter 8.)

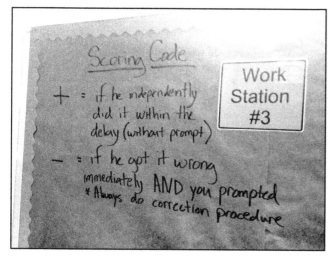

Figure 1.13. Visual reminder.
Jenny posted this visual reminder to staff in a 1-1 instructional area of how to take the data and the code that is used for particular students.

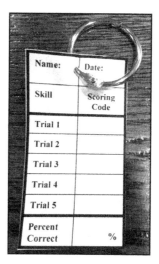

Figure 1.14. Keychain.
Jenny made a keychain for data collection for easy portability when the students go into the community.

Classroom Zoning Plan — Senior High School

Time / Activity	Jenny	Barbara	Sal	Comments/ Contingency Plans
7:15-8:00 Breakfast/ Clean Cafeteria	Check setup of individual and group schedules.	Meet students at cafeteria and supervise breakfast and table washing. Take data on one student per day on naturalistic data sheet.	Meet students at cafeteria and supervise breakfast and table washing.	
8:00-8:20 Morning Meeting	Run morning meeting with whole group.	Assist with morning meeting, prompting from behind nonverbally. Take data on one student per day on naturalistic data sheet.	Set up centers, make sure IW is set up for first set of centers.	
8:20-8:40 Center 1	Reading with Corey and Phillip. Trial-by-trial data daily and work product.	Monitor computer and Language Master with Trent, Carter, and Sharon. Take data on one student per day on naturalistic data sheet.	Facilitate IW with Dontel, Kai, and Spence. Use IW data sheet to take data on one student each day.	
8:40-9:00 Center 2	Reading with Trent, Carter, and Sharon. Trial-by-trial data daily and work product.	Monitor computer and Language Master with Dontel, Kai, and Spence. Take data on one student per day on naturalistic data sheet.	Facilitate IW with Corey and Phillip. Use IW data sheet to take data on one student each day.	
9:00-9:20 Center 3	Reading with Dontel, Kai, and Spence. Trial-by-trial data daily and work product.	Monitor computer with Corey and Phillip. Take data on one student per day on naturalistic data sheet.	IW with Trent, Carter, and Sharon. Use IW data sheet to take data on one student each day.	
9:20-10:15 PE	Planning time.	PE with the students. Take data on one student per day on naturalistic data sheet.	PE with the students. Take data on one student per day on naturalistic data sheet.	
10:15-10:30 Center 4	Math with Corey and Phillip. Trial-by-trial data and work product.	IW with Trent, Carter, and Sharon. Take data on one student per day on naturalistic data sheet.	Vocational with Dontel, Kai, and Spence. Take data on one student per day on naturalistic data sheet.	
10:30-10:45 Center 5	Math with Dontel, Kai, and S. Trial-by-trial data and work product.	IW with Corey and Phillip. Take data on one student per day on naturalistic data sheet.	Vocational with Trent, Carter, and Sharon. Take data on one student per day on naturalistic data sheet.	
10:45-11:00 Center 6	Math with Trent, Carter, and Sharon. Trial-by-trial data and work product.	IW with Dontel and Spence. Weekly data collection on each student.	Vocational with Corey and Phillip. Take data on one student per day.	Kai goes to lunch.

Figure 1.15. Zoning plan.
Jenny's zoning plan allows her to assign data collection responsibilities across the day to each staff member involved. This ensures that data is collected regularly and that each staff member knows when it is her turn.

TASK ANALYSIS DATA SHEET WITH METHOD

Skill: cleans cafeteria	**Student's Name:**
Area: vocational	**Primary Instructor:**
Direction: "Time to clean the tables"	**Setting:** Cafeteria
Target Behavior: wiping tables and counters	**Prerequisites:** follow 1-step directions

Date:								
Criterion Prompt								
Criterion Step:								
Record the prompting level in each box.								

Step	Method								
Gets materials with list	Gets cloth, spray bottle								
Goes to designated area for cleaning	Tell him what room he is cleaning tables in								
Sprays left side of table	Point to area to spray								
Wipes where he sprayed	Point to where to wipe; make sure he wipes up all the water								
Sprays right side of table	Point to area to spray								
Wipes where he sprayed	Point to where to wipe; make sure he wipes up all the water								
Sprays counter 1	Point to counter and tell him to spray counter								
Wipes counter 1	Point to counter								
Sprays counter 2	Point to counter and tell him to spray counter								
Wipes counter 2	Point to counter								
Puts away materials	Point to his schedule and use nonverbal cues to have him clean up								
Staff Initials:									
Level of Mastery:									

Scoring Code:	S-Visual	Comments/Observations:
+ Correct	V-Verbal prompt from a distance	___/___/ _____
X Incorrect	0-Does not perform step	___/___/ _____
P-Physical		___/___/ _____
G-Gestural		

Criterion for Mastery:	Materials:

Adapted from Nova Southeastern University Autism Programs. Used with permission.

Figure 1.16. Task analysis data sheet.

For students working on self-help skills, Jenny's staff uses a task analysis data sheet to remind them of the steps and allow data collection on independent performance for each step.

Incredible 5-Point Scale
Self-Monitoring

Name:		Date:	

This is how I am feeling at the start of the period.

1 = I am really glad to be here. I will participate and I may even be able to help others.
2 = I am glad to be here and I will participate.
3 = I am here but I might not participate.
4 = I am here but I will not participate. I will not disrupt.
5 = I will not participate and I may disrupt if I have to stay in the room.

	Monday	Tuesday	Wednesday	Thursday	Friday
Period 1					
Period 2					
Period 3					
Period 4					
Period 5					
Period 6					
Period 7					
Comments					

Figure 1.17. Self-regulation data sheet.

Jenny uses the Incredible 5-Point Scale (Buron & Curtis, 2012) to teach students self-regulation. This data sheet requires each student to rate his or her ability to participate at the beginning of an activity and allows students to track their own data over time.

Work Sample Data Collection

Setting: (circle 1)   Sp.Ed.   Gen. Ed.   Speech   OT

Other_____

____ Independent (nothing else should be checked)
____ Physical proximity of adult ONLY
____ Prompting for initial performance ONLY

PROMPTING (Check all that apply)

Visual	_____	Gestural	_____
Model	_____	Verbal	_____
Physical	_____	Notes:	_____

Date: _____   Staff Initials: _____

Figure 1.18. Label.

Jenny uses this work sample data label that can be completed by staff and attached to permanent products to allow for quick and easy data collection in the community and the classroom.

Daily Job Training
How Did I Do Today?

Name:	Date:
Job Site:	On-site Supervisor:
School Job Coach:	

Rating Scale:
3 Excellent (e.g., independent, high quality)
2 Adequate (e.g., some prompts, acceptable quality)
1 Poor (e.g., did not complete, needed significant help, poor quality)

Skill Acquisition	My Rating	On-site Supervisor	School Job Coach	Comments
Begins work				
Follows directions from supervisor				
Asks for help when needed				
Quality of work				
Pace of work				
Interacts with coworkers				
Other skill				

Figure 1.19. Daily rating sheet.

Out in the community, this sheet allows the job coach, supervisor, and the worker to rate the worker's performance, ideally leading to self-monitoring for the worker. It also provides Jenny with an effective data collection system on the work site.

Basic Communication Rubric: Listening Skills

Name:	Date:
Activity:	Rater:

Circle the appropriate indicator for each behavior.

Behavior	0	1	2	3	4	Points Received
Uses eye gaze appropriately	Does not look at person talking when prompted	Looks at person talking when prompted	Looks at person talking for brief moment	Looks at person talking for sustained period	Shifts gaze appropriately towards communication partner	
Responds on topic	Does not respond	Responds on a different topic or responds on topic when prompted	Responds on topic 50% of the time	Responds on topic 75% of the time	Responds on topic 100% of the time	
Waits his or her turn to talk/doesn't interrupt	Does not wait for his/her turn; Interrupts	Needs prompt or cue to wait for his/her turn; Does not interrupt	Waits his or her turn to talk 50% of the time	Waits his or her turn to talk 75% of the time	Waits his or her turn to talk 100% of the time	

0	1	2	3	4
No success, even with help	Partial success at the 2.0 or 3.0 level with help	Independent success at 2.0 level	Independent success at 3.0 level	Independent success with more complex skill

Based on Marzano, R. J. (2010). *Formative assessment and standards-based grading.* Bloomington, IN: Marzano Resarch Laboratory.

Figure 1.20. Rubric.

Jenny uses a rubric to assess social skills in the community and the classroom. The rubric can be completed once a week by a classroom staff member or a job coach.

Data collection is a challenging but critically important component of instruction. Teachers know they need to take data, but they don't always know how to make sure the information they need to make good decisions about student performance is collected. Consequently, many teachers take extensive data and feel overwhelmed by the thought of having to summarize it, while many others take too little data and then don't have the information they need to make effective decisions about their students' progress.

Research indicates that teachers report taking data but using it inconsistently or feeling that the data was not an accurate representation of what the students were able to do (Sandall, Schwartz, & LaCroix, 2004). One of the most frequent concerns of teachers is trying to take data without feeling that the collection process itself interferes with their instruction. This book was written to solve this problem! It provides examples and guidelines for developing and implementing systems for data collection and data analysis and presents practical strategies for implementing effective practices within a variety of classroom and community settings.

About This Book

Throughout the book, we refer to skill acquisition data and challenging behavior data. Skill acquisition data is intended to include data for skills that are being taught, whether as part of IEP goals and objectives or skills that are taught as part of the curriculum. These skills can include academic skills, functional skills, speech and language skills, social and behavioral skills, and skills needed to perform jobs and activities in the community. For the purposes of this book, challenging behavior data includes any assessment of behaviors that interfere with learning or performance across a variety of settings. Although some of the same strategies can be used to collect data on both challenging behavior and skill acquisition, for clarity we will discuss them as separate processes in the upcoming chapters.

In Chapter 2, we discuss methods for planning how to take skill acquisition data within the context of a classroom, a work site, a community setting, or any other situation in which an instructor is managing multiple responsibilities. We will talk about how to determine what data is needed as well as ways to match types of data collection with the skill being targeted.

In Chapter 3, we review a variety of data collection strategies and formats for collecting data on students' progress on IEP goals and objectives as well as curriculum skills. The chapter includes an overview of the different types of data that may be helpful (e.g., rate data, samples of data) as well as examples of forms.

Chapter 4 focuses on guidelines and ways to quickly summarize and analyze skill acquisition data, make decisions about progress, and address problems with learning. We move to discussing data for challenging behavior in Chapter 5, when we review making decisions about the types of data needed as well as different forms and strategies for collecting data on interfering or problematic behaviors. Then, in Chapter 6 we share some strategies for summarizing and analyzing the data on challenging behavior. Coming back to the topic of how to fit data collection into the natural environment, Chapter 7 focuses specifically on organizational strategies we have found useful for managing data collection in the natural environment.

In Chapter 8, we revisit Sally, Sam, and Jenny, our three instructors from the case studies, to demonstrate how they planned data collection for their respective settings. Finally, Chapter 9 highlights answers to frequently asked questions we have encountered from instructors in relation to their data collection and analysis challenges.

> **Please Note:** All of the forms discussed throughout the book will be available electronically at
> https://www.aapcpublishing.net/bookstore/books/9123.aspx
> for easy adaptation to your needs.

Chapter 2
Planning for Data Collection for Skill Acquisition

Overview

A number of factors affect selection of a data strategy, including:

- What type of skill is being assessed (e.g., handwriting, reading comprehension)?

- How is the IEP goal/objective or curriculum skill written (e.g., criteria for mastery)?

- Where is the behavior or skill being demonstrated (e.g., classroom, worksite)?

- Who is available to take data in a given setting (e.g., only one instructor, multiple support staff)?

A review of tools for supporting and planning data collection, including a classroom zoning plan (e.g., staff schedule) and the CAPS with examples, will be provided in this chapter.

Data need to be collected in a way that provides accurate and reliable measurements of the target skill – whether the skill is the focus of an IEP goal or a skill in a curriculum that all students are expected to master. Accurate measurement ensures that the skill being measured is the one that is being targeted. For instance, a word problem test designed to only assess addition would not be an accurate assessment because it would not address the reading and the computation skills required for the task.

Further, reliable measurement is achieved when the measurement tool can assess the skill the same way each time. For instance, if two educators observe morning meeting to assess a student's ability to answer questions, and one educator reports that the student answered three questions and the other reports that he answered five questions, the measurement system is clearly not reliable. Ensuring that the data collected is reliable and accurate requires making several decisions in planning.

1. What type of skill is being assessed? Different skills lend themselves to different types of measurement dependent upon how the skill looks and how frequently it occurs.

2. How is the IEP goal or curriculum skill and its mastery criteria written? The way the educational team has determined that the student will show mastery of the skill affects the type of data needed to make that decision (e.g., 100 words/minute, remains in a group activity for 20 minutes).

3. Where will the skill be exhibited and measured?

4. What staff will be available to collect the data when it needs to be collected?

What Type of Skill Is Being Assessed?

The first consideration in determining what type of data needs to be collected relates to the skill that is being assessed. For instance, some skills, such as mastery of spelling words, lend themselves to being measured using tests. Others, like communication skills, need to be observed in the natural environment.

Table 2.1 outlines how different types of data lend themselves to specific types of skills. For example, writing, whether the focus is on handwriting or composing a narrative using written language, lends itself best to work samples that are assessed through some type of standard rubric. Typically, writing is analyzed to determine if it meets the criteria required for mastery based upon whether it contains certain elements. Consequently, the grader is typically using some type of rubric or pre-set criteria to determine if the sample of the writing on the test meets the requirements.

TABLE 2.1

Matching Skill to Type of Data

Subject Area	Targeted Skill	Type of Data Collected
Handwriting	Handwriting	Permanent product (writing sample) — assessed with rubric
	Written narratives	Permanent product (writing sample) — assessed with rubric
Reading	Comprehension	Permanent product (test graded for accuracy or label on work sample)
	Fluency	Event recording — rate (words read correctly/minute)
	Decoding	Event recording — frequency/accuracy (e.g., read third-grade paragraph with three or fewer errors)
Math	Comprehension	Permanent product (test graded for accuracy or label on work sample)
	Fluency	Event recording — rate (completed _____ problems/minute)
	Solving word problems	Permanent product (test graded for accuracy or label on work sample) (solve _____ type of word problem with 80% accuracy or identify key words in story problems with 80% accuracy)
Social skills	Quantity of individual skills (e.g., initiation of interaction, responding to others)	Event recording — frequency or rate for specific time periods (e.g., snack)
	Quality of interactions (e.g., balanced turn taking in a conversation)	Rubric or checklist completed weekly
	Length of interactions (e.g., time spent in group activity)	Time-based recording — duration
Communication	Quantity of individual skills (e.g., initiation of interaction, responding to others)	Event recording — frequency or rate for specific time periods (e.g., snack) Event recording — event-by-event
	Length of communicative interaction (e.g., conversation)	Event recording — frequency (e.g., number of turns) Time-based recording — duration
	Quality of interactions (e.g., maintaining appropriate distance from communication partner)	Rubric or checklist completed weekly
Self-care skills/job performance	Completion of task (e.g., setting the table, brushing teeth)	Checklist/task analysis, as in Figure 1.7
Toileting	Completion of routine	Checklist/task analysis, as in Figure 3.10
	Number of accidents/dry pants	Event recording — frequency or rate of accidents
	Recording when toileting accidents occur or when individual produces in the toilet	Event recording — scatterplot
Independent work/functional routines	Task analysis of steps of task (e.g., independent work system)	Checklist/task analysis, as in Figure 3.8
Learning readiness skills (following directions, sitting, imitating, responding to name)	Percent trials correct	Event recording — discrete trial data sheets

How Is the IEP Goal/Objective or Curriculum Skill Written?

Data in school settings are typically collected to determine if a student mastered the skills in the curriculum or IEP goals/objectives. Therefore, how the targeted skill is written – whether an element of the curriculum or a component of the IEP – is a critical consideration in determining what data is needed to determine mastery.

In IEPs, it is typical to write an overarching annual measurable goal with several measurable objectives. The objectives are either benchmarks along the way to achieving mastery of the goal or subskills that are necessary to master the goal at progressive times so that the student reaches the overall goal.

Goal:

By the end of the year, Bonnie will independently access goods and services in 3 community settings and interact appropriately, saying "thank you" and "you're welcome" in response to natural environmental/social cues with relevant personnel using scripts and predictable routines as observed by her SLP on 3 different occasions.

Objective:

By the end of the first grading period, Bonnie will independently check out materials at her neighborhood library and interact with library personnel using a script and predictable routine at least 3 times.

By the end of the second grading period, Bonnie will independently purchase a treat and interact with the personnel at her local coffee shop using a script and predictable routine at least 3 times.

By the end of the third grading period, Bonnie will independently purchase items from a list and interact with the personnel at her local drugstore using a script and predictable routine at least 3 times.

Figure 2.1. Example of goal and objectives from an IEP or habilitation plan.

The practice of reporting progress on IEP goals and objectives differs across states and even districts. For example, in the authors' district, at the preschool level, quarterly progress is only reported on the goal, although the instruction is based on the objectives and data are collected on the component objectives. In a different state in which the authors work, progress reports contain information about performance on both the goal and the component objectives. In general, for students who are working towards the standards, only measureable goals are written. For students working toward alternate standards, both goals and objectives are needed.

When goals and objectives are poorly written, it is difficult to take accurate data because there is limited agreement on the skill that is to be assessed. Further, goals or objectives containing several component skills are also difficult to assess for mastery because the student may have mastered one of the components but not the others, and, as a result, would have to be rated as not having mastered the skill.

There are generally three elements to writing annual goals. The first contains the information about the conditions under which the skill will be demonstrated, such as whether visual cues are provided, the size of the group in which the student is expected to demonstrate the skill, the prompting level with which the student is expected to perform the skill, or the type of materials the student uses to demonstrate the skill.

The second element is the actual skill written in behavioral terms so that it is clear what skill is being targeted. Examples of clearly written skills include adding two single-digit numbers from 0 to 9; writing a statement that includes a subject, verb, and object that begins with a capital and ends with a period; or answering "who" questions about a kindergarten-level story heard.

The last element of a goal or behavioral objective involves the criteria for mastery. Examples of criteria include percent correct, number of demonstrations of the skill compared to the number of opportunities for the skill to be demonstrated in a 15-minute period, or a score on a rubric out of total points possible. Such information allows the teacher to make clear decisions about whether the student has mastered the skill as written.

> **Goal:**
> Bonnie will independently access goods and services and interact appropriately, saying "thank you" and "you're welcome" in response to natural environmental/social cues with relevant personnel in 3 community settings using scripts and predictable routines as observed by her SLP on 3 different occasions by the end of the year.
>
> **Information and conditions under which the skill will be demonstrated:**
> Independently, in 3 community settings using scripts and predictable routines.
>
> **Clear, objective skills to be demonstrated:**
> Access goods and services and interact appropriately, saying "thank you" and "you're welcome" in response to natural environmental/social cues with relevant personnel.
>
> **Criteria for mastery:**
> As observed by her SLP on 3 different occasions by the end of the year.

Figure 2.2. Goal for an IEP or habilitation plan highlighting the three elements of objective, measurable goals.

What Is the Difference Between Well-Written and Unclear Goals/Objectives?

It is difficult to write high-quality goals and objectives. Careful attention must be paid to making the conditions, skill, and criteria clear to the person who is responsible for the student's program implementation. There are often problems in understanding when a teacher inherits an IEP from another district or teacher, or from an evaluation team. The following are examples of ambiguous goals/objectives.

1. **"Andy will (a) choose a game/toy, (b) choose a friend, (c) play with peers appropriately at 60-70% mastery by the end of the school year."**

This statement contains many problems. First, it does not include information about the conditions under which the skill must be performed (i.e., is an adult providing supervision or prompting, are visual supports being used to help the student make his choices, or does the student need a speech generating device to communicate with the peer during play?). Second, the statement contains three different skills, which means that the student may master one of the component skills, but not the two others. In that case, he will not get credit for mastering the whole objective. If this statement were a goal, it would be important for each of the three skills listed to be included as objectives under the goal. The mastery level is stated as 60-70% by the end of the school year, so it may be assumed that the statement is either a goal or the last objective to be met towards the end of the school year after other objectives are mastered. Third, since the behaviors of choosing a toy, choosing a peer, and playing appropriately would all be measured by a staff member observing the behavior occur, it is more useful to talk about the first two as number of successful choices among the number of opportunities presented, which can be turned into a percent. Fourth, it would also be important to limit the count to a specified timeframe, so that the staff knows how often this occurs in a 15-minute playtime. Fifth, the third skill talks about playing appropriately. The word "appropriately" involves a subjective rating by the observer, and it may be difficult to get two individuals to agree on whether the play is appropriate. It would be better to use a clearer, behavioral definition of "appropriate play," like "share materials," "take turns during a board game," or "assign and take roles when in the pretend play area." An alternative goal for the same skill would be:

Goal: Given visual supports, Andy will choose a friend and sustain an interaction with a peer for 15 minutes during a structured play activity on 8/10 observations.

Objective 1: Given visual supports, Andy will choose a toy using a picture communication symbol and play independently for 15 minutes during a structured play time on 8/10 observations.

Objective 2: Given visual supports, Andy will choose a friend and ask the friend to play with his chosen toy or game using a picture communication symbol during a structured play activity on 8/10 observations.

Objective 3: Given visual supports, Andy will play with a chosen peer and game or toy for 10 minutes during a structured play activity on 8/10 opportunities.

2. "Andy will participate in social skills training at 50-60% mastery by the end of the school year."

This goal/objective is also ambiguous for a number of reasons. First, no conditions are stated to let the teacher know how the skill is to be performed. Participating in social skills training does not define the actual skill that is being targeted, so it is enough for the student to attend the social skills group and do something, but the teacher is not sure what that is. Second, it is difficult to know what a mastery criterion of 50-60% is when we don't know what skill we are measuring. The way this is written allows the teacher to draw the conclusion that if the student attends 5 out of 10 social skills classes and participates in them or attends all of them and participates in five out of 10 social skills classes, he has reached mastery. A better alternative would be the following:

Goal: Andy will participate during 30-minute social skills groups by answering questions with relevant answers and following teacher directions for 4/5 groups within a month.

3. "Andy will interactively play with age-appropriate peers and items at 60-70% mastery by the end of the school year."

Again, this goal/objective is ambiguous. First, the reader can assume that this is an annual goal because mastery is supposed to occur by the end of the year. No conditions are defined. For instance, is this done during structured or unstructured activities or are visual supports used? Second, the skill is stated as "interactive play with age-appropriate peers." Are these same-aged peers who are in a special education classroom with the student or in a general education classroom? Are they classmates or just out on the playground at the same time? Third, what constitutes "interactive play?" The target would be much clearer if it was written as, "The student will verbally initiate a pretend-play game on the playground or in the play area" or "The student will respond to a peer's invitation to take a role in a pretend-play game on the playground or in the play area." Fourth, does mastery involve doing the skill 6 out of 10 days or 6 out of 10 opportunities presented? A better alternative goal for this example would be the example below.

Goal: Given visual supports, Andy will choose a friend and sustain an interaction with a peer for 15 minutes during a structured play activity on 8/10 observations.

Where Is the Behavior or Skill Being Demonstrated?

When writing an IEP goal/objective, it is important to decide where the skill/behavior is to be used. Some goals/objectives naturally fit into certain environments in a school setting. For example, gross-motor skills may be best written to be demonstrated on playground equipment; social-language skills may be targeted in a general education setting or in the cafeteria, and eating/feeding skills may best be demonstrated in the cafeteria; new pre-academic skills may best be performed in a small-group setting within the classroom; and mobility skills for a high school student may best be mastered during class change times in the hallways.

Who Is Available to Take Data in a Given Setting?

It is critically important to train all of the instructional staff to take data on different types of skills using a variety of data collection procedures. The assignment of data collection responsibilities should always be made by the teacher and be contained in the classroom zoning plan. A zoning plan is basically a staff schedule that defines what each of the classroom staff is assigned to do across the entire day in terms of students they are responsible for, activities they are leading or serving a support function for, and where they should be in the classroom. Additional duties like cleaning up, setting up activities, taking children to the bathroom, ensuring the lunch count gets to the office, and taking data should all be defined as part of the zoning plan. Figure 2.3 presents an example of a zoning plan where data collection is assigned.

Sally's Zoning Plan (Excerpt)

Time/Activity	Sally	Chrissy	Robert	Comments
7:30-8:15 Arrival/Breakfast	Start at cafeteria; bring back N and S, bathroom students as you are able	Start at cafeteria, remain in cafeteria until all students have arrived; then escort students to room	Start at cafeteria, remain in cafeteria until all students or most of students have arrived, then escort to class	
8:15-8:30 Table Tasks	Transition first students back to schedule and table tasks; man table tasks; take data on two students' targeted goals each day	Transition students back to classroom, check their schedule, and check into table tasks; begin to pull students for bathroom one to two at a time; toileting data for B and S	Transition students back to classroom, check their schedule, and check into table tasks; begin to pull students for bathroom one to two at a time; toileting data for B and S	
8:30-8:45 Journals	Supervise journals, help students complete their page and tell about it if they can	Continue to pull students to bathroom and assist with journals when available	Continue to pull students to bathroom and assist with journals when available	Work product data collection
8:45-9:00 Circle	Run circle	Prompt and assist all students, particularly S; take data on one designated student's targeted goals/day	Prompt and assist all students, particularly N; take data on one designated student's targeted goals/day	
9:00-9:15 Centers 1	Reading with C and S; take daily data	Individual work with B and A; take data on one student per day	Art with N and N; take data on one student per day	
9:15-9:30 Centers 2	Reading with N and N; take daily data	IW with C and S; take data on one student per day	Art with B and A; take data on one student per day	
9:30-9:45 Centers 3	Reading with B and A; take daily data	IW with N and N; set up table tasks; take data on one student per day	Art with C and S; take data on one student per day	Mon and Thurs C goes to speech
9:45-10:00 TT/BR	Pull students 1-2 at a time for bathroom; toileting data for B and S	Pull students 1-2 at a time for bathroom; toileting data for B and S	Supervise table tasks	
10:00-10:30 PE/Gym	Stay to make sure choice time is ready, then join PE	Accompany students to PE; take data on one student per day	Accompany students to PE; take data on one student per day	

Figure 2.3. Zoning plan.

The zoning plan serves as a staff schedule and list of duties for Sally's classroom. The screened elements highlight when data is collected and by whom.

If a paraprofessional is responsible for accompanying a student to the general education setting, he or she must be trained about what type of data to obtain, including the need for adult prompts to complete work, to stay in the assigned seat, or to respond to a peer's initiation, if those are targeted skills. It is also important for the paraprofessional to be able to evaluate the type of assistance the student needs to complete assignments like worksheets and to assess the accuracy of work completed. The CAPS can be useful in providing information about how this should be evaluated.

Use of the Comprehensive Autism Planning System (CAPS) to Communicate Data Collection Protocols

One of the tools that is useful when organizing the data collection process for an individual student in a school setting is the Comprehensive Autism Planning System (CAPS; Henry & Myles, 2013). Multiple versions of the CAPS have been developed to meet particular needs. We have found the original CAPS to be useful for students with ASD who are being included in general education classrooms. The CAPS-teaching plan (CAPS-TP) was developed by the authors to assist in the organization of classroom environments for students receiving education in more specialized settings. With the CAPS-TP, the teacher begins the process with students' individual goals and objectives, while the traditional CAPS is organized around the schedule of the day. Figure 2.4 shows a CAPS-TP for a first grader.

Calen's CAPS reflects how his IEP is to be implemented across his day. It includes the type of data that is collected and how often data should be collected for each objective on his IEP.

Comprehensive Autism Planning System (CAPS)/Teaching Plan

Student: Calen Barber	Common Reinforcers (*embedded throughout the day*) Computer time, iPad, reading a story with the teacher, beanbag chair
Communication System: Gestures, pictures and symbols and some limited signs	Sensory Strategies (*embedded throughout the day*) Frequent breaks through the day—about every 20 minutes
Date Completed: 8/24/15	Case Manager / Teacher: Sally McKenzie
Grade: 1st	School Year: 2015-2016

For students served primarily in self-contained classrooms or as part of the process for designing a self-contained classroom, begin completing the following grid with the student's IEP and curriculum objectives to build the schedule. For students who are primarily participating in a general education classroom, you might start with the schedule column and target the goals/skills from that, completing the rest of the grid as needed.

Goal/Objective/ Targeted Skill	Primary Teaching Activity/ Scheduled Activity	Teaching Strategy	Structure/ Modifications/ Accommodations	Reinforcers	Communication/ Social Supports	Data Collection	Generalization Plan
Calen will isolate the initial sound of five words, with 80% accuracy by the end of October 2015.	Reading	Unique Learning System Lesson 10 Word Study	Visual cues; wait time	Token board	PECS book	ULS monthly checkpoint assessments	Reading stories
By January 2016, Calen will recognize 10 kindergarten high-frequency words in print from a basal reader word list with 90% accuracy.	Reading	Discrete trials—sight words STAR Level 2 Pre-academic Lesson 11	Visual cues; wait time	Token board	PECS book	Self-graphing discrete trial data sheet	Morning meeting
Calen will match consonant and vowel sounds to five letters, with 80% accuracy by the end of May 2016.	Reading	Discrete Trials Receptive ID of Letter Sounds	Visual cues; wait time	Token board	PECS book	Self-graphing discrete trial data sheet	Reading word wall

Created by Reeve and Kabot. Modified from Henry, S.A., & Myles, B.S. (2013). *The Comprehensive Autism Planning System (CAPS) for individuals with autism spectrum and related disabilities: Integrating evidence-based practices throughout the student's day* (2nd ed.). Shawnee Mission, KS: AAPC Publishing.

Figure 2.4. CAPS - TP.

In this example the objectives are listed because they are subskills of the goal. When the objectives are benchmarks of the goal, the operationalization takes place around the goal since the benchmarks are basically the same but with different criteria. When the objectives are subskills of the goal, the operationalization takes place for each of the subskills, as in this example. The primary teaching activity is where data collection takes place, while the generalization plan may present other places to practice the skill throughout the day; but during the acquisition phase, data is not necessarily taken in those other settings. The CAPS presents the teaching strategy or technique that is being used to teach the skill and may include discrete trial teaching (DTT), task analysis, pivotal response training (PRT), or techniques embedded in specific curricula (e.g., Unique Learning System; ULS; https://www.n2y.com/products/unique).

There is a place to list the environmental structure the student needs to be successful, as well as modifications and accommodations that are being provided. A modification is a change to what is taught and may be to spell five weekly spelling words when other students are responsible for the complete list of 10; an accommodation is a change to how something is taught and may be to spell the words orally instead of on a written test. Reinforcers that are exceptionally powerful for the student during this activity or for this skill are listed so that the teaching staff know what they should have available when instructing the student on this goal/objective. There is a space to describe any communication or social supports the student needs to learn the skill, such as visual supports and augmentative communication tools.

It is important to consider multiple factors when determining what data collection systems need to be put into place. Once you have an understanding of the instructional targets for each individual you are responsible for, you can select data collection instruments and methods that match the needs of the person using the information provided in Chapter 3.

Chapter 3
Data Collection for Skill Acquisition

Overview

There are many options available for data collection instruments and procedures for skill acquisition. This chapter provides information to help you make decisions about what data collection form will be best for your situation.

- Can you keep a permanent product that the student creates and provide information about the support or conditions under which the work was completed?

- Is the skill taught in isolation or embedded into a classroom activity or routine?

- Do you have the opportunity to take data for students in a group or are you taking data for one student at a time?

- Is taking a sample of data enough or do you need to take information about each production of a skill?

Different types of data collection are needed to assess the myriad skills that make up a student's educational program. Essentially, two categories of quantitative data collection methods may be used to evaluate a student's learning: permanent products and quantified performance observations.

Permanent Products

Permanent products encompass any type of concrete material that can be evaluated and on which performance can be compared over time. As such, a permanent product includes tests, worksheets, writing samples, and any other activity that results in a product that can be saved, evaluated, and compared.

There are a variety of factors you need to consider when using a permanent product to evaluate learning of a skill. First, it is important that the skills that are compared are the same. For instance, if you are evaluating a student's ability to cut, it is important to compare samples of cutting a circle with other examples of cutting a circle, since comparing circle cutting to cutting on a straight line would not be a valid comparison.

Second, it is important that the conditions under which you take the samples are uniform. For instance, if the student is completing a science experiment with a partner, it would not be a good comparison to a science experiment that was completed alone. Third, it is important to retain work samples on a regular and systematic basis. This keeps you from selecting only good (or poor) samples and reduces bias in the way the work samples were selected.

Permanent products are typically assessed by grading them, using either a percentage of correct answers for quantitative measures of accuracy (with or without grade cutoffs) or a rubric for more qualitative skills such as writing. In the latter case, the rubric serves to turn more qualitative information into a quantitative measure of performance. In both cases the assessment typically results in a graded score.

In addition to retaining the work sample or other permanent product, it is important to record the context in which the student completed it. For example, did he receive prompting to write his name? Was the test provided with extra time or in a 1-1 setting? This type of information allows you to assess the student's performance changes over time with all the relevant variables.

Work Sample Label

To ensure that contextual information is recorded and saved with the work sample, we have found it useful to use preprinted labels with places to fill in or check off the necessary information. When using the label, first circle the setting in which the sample was completed. Next, if the student completed the work sample with no assistance, you would check "Independent" — nothing else would be checked off. If the student did not complete the skill completely independently, indicate if the student needed to have an adult in the proximity of her work area or whether she needed assistance just to start the task. If neither of those applies, you check off the type of assistance the student needed to complete the work. If the student needed more than one type of assistance (e.g., a model and a verbal prompt) you can record more than one by checking multiple types of prompts. You then write in the date and your initials (so that more information can be sought later from the person completing the label). Finally, peel the label off the sheet and paste it onto the student's work sample in a blank space or on the back of the page.

Below is an example of a label that we have used to record work performance. An electronic copy of this label can be obtained at https://www.aapcpublishing.net/bookstore/books/9123.aspx and can be printed on a standard shipping label (3.33 x 4").

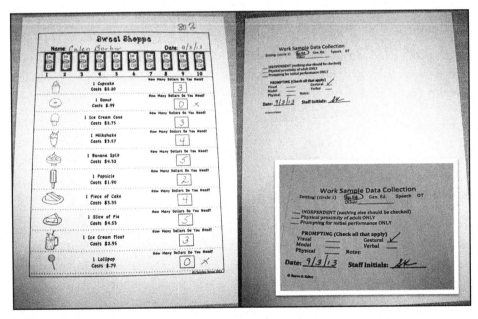

Figure 3.1. Work sample label.
The data was collected in the special education setting and the student required gestural prompts to complete the task to which the label is affixed.

Rubric. Rubrics are commonly used for evaluating writing samples and projects in the classroom when it is not possible to grade a work product by directly assigning a numerical score, like the percent of correct answers on a test or the percent of correct answers to math problems on a worksheet.

Rubrics (see Figure 3.2) are developed by assigning a numerical rating scale to define elements of a work product. The most common rubric used in schools today reflects the model promoted by Marzano (2010), which uses a 4-point scale beginning with 0.0. (Adaptations of the scale add 1/2 point criteria.) With his scale, a score of 3.0 generally indicates mastery of the target learning goal. Mastery of more complex content receives a score of 4.0, whereas mastery of simpler content receives a score of 2.0. A score of 1.0 means that a student needed help to be successful with any of the content and has not mastered the content independently. A score of 0.0 indicates that the student is not successful with any of the content at a 2.0 or 3.0 level, even with assistance.

Rubric for Informative Essay

	4	3	2	1
Focus	Very clear and creative statement of main idea, communicated throughout the essay	Clear statement of main idea, communicated throughout the essay	Unclear focus on a main idea, unfocused paragraphs	No focus on any main idea
Organization	Creative introduction and conclusion, use of transitions and logical progression of ideas	Good introduction and conclusion, use of transitions and logical progression of ideas	Weak introduction and conclusion, weak use of transitions, no logical progression of ideas	No clear organization and difficult to understand
Elaboration	Strong use of sources, facts, and details to support the main statement	Good use of sources, facts, and details to support the main statement	Weak introduction and conclusion, weak use of transitions, no logical progression of ideas	Much more detail needed to support this writing
Language	Creative and strong use of words to express ideas and share facts	Good use of words to express ideas and share facts	Word choice is weak, ideas and facts are hard to understand	Words do not show ideas or facts at all
Conventions	Strong use of paragraphs, complete sentences, quotes, capitals, punctuation, spelling	Some errors in conventions, but errors do not interfere with understanding the essay	Many errors, making the essay hard to understand	Severe errors, making the essay very hard to understand

Used with permission from Retta London of Rainbow City Learning http://www.teacherspayteachers.com/Store/Rainbow-City-Learning.

Figure 3.2. Commercially available rubric for writing an informative essay using the scale from Marzano (2010).

Another way to conceptualize a rubric is to follow the scale that matches the Unique Learning System (ULS) (https://www.n2y.com/products/unique), which looks at Independent, Supported, and Participatory involvement in an activity. This framework assigns a number to the student's involvement in the activity when there is not a product to grade. A 4-point scale would be used to rate the student's achievement in a learning activity.

3.0	Independent involvement in the activity
2.0	Supported involvement in the activity
1.0	Participatory involvement in the activity
0.0	No involvement in the activity

Figure 3.3. Example of rubric used in the ULS.

Tests. Another type of permanent product is tests, which take a variety of forms throughout a school. State standardized tests evaluate students' performance compared to other students in the classroom, district, and state. These tests are provided under strict conditions with established procedures to ensure consistency in the data collected.

The more common form of tests that teachers use to regularly assess progress includes publisher-created curriculum-based assessments and teacher-made tests. Curriculum-based assessments typically entail using standardized methods to collect the information on the given test to ensure comparability of performance on the test across time.

In order to ensure consistent measurement of skills over time, it is important to develop teacher-made tests, such as chapter tests or spelling tests, in a standard way. In other words, spelling tests should always involve the teacher saying the word to be spelled and using it in a sentence so that the students' scores can be compared over time. Most textbooks and other resources come with tests that are developed in a consistent manner.

When giving tests, it is important to have set procedures regarding the assistance provided (e.g., whether prompting is used to keep a student on task during the test) and the use of modifications or accommodations to meet individual student needs. Be sure to record this information with the results of the test to ensure that scores across time are comparable. If the test protocol or format does not include the students' answers with a copy of the test, save the test form for reference if there are questions about the students' performance. In a general education classroom, this might involve recording the grades or scores in a gradebook, keeping the original test given to the students, and possibly saving copies of the students' answer sheets for the year or saving copies of the tests of students who received accommodations, modifications, or assistance of some kind. This enables the educational team to review the data to compare the student's performance over time and ensure that all the information needed is available. Tests usually result in scores that translate into grades. If the test questions are open-ended, there is typically a guide for grading that gives information about standards required to receive credit, similar to a rubric.

Quantified Performance Observations

Quantified performance observations include any type of data that requires a person to observe a behavior or skill and record it in a consistent and objective manner. Typically, the measurements in this category fall into two major groups – event and time recording (Cooper, Heron, & Heward, 2007).

Event recording. Event recording includes frequency and rate data, event-by-event recording, and checklist or task analysis data.

Frequency and rate data. Frequency data involves counting each time a specific skill is demonstrated. When trying to assess a student's initiations of social interactions with a peer, for example, a teacher might use a counter or pencil and paper to tally the number of times the student approached another child and started an interaction. Typically, you need to have uninterrupted time to observe the student's behavior when taking frequency data and the opportunity to record data as the behavior occurs. The data then yields a count of instances of the skill observed and can be compared with other observations. However, if the observations are of different lengths, the data will not be comparable. To make the data comparable, you would convert the frequency to rate data.

Rate data gives frequency within specific time parameters. It is best used when observation sessions are not likely to be the same length, which frequently occurs in classroom situations. This means that in addition to recording the count of the skill being observed, you should record how long your observation lasted so that you can calculate the rate for comparison to other observations. One key to successful frequency and rate data collection is ensuring that you are able to observe and record each instance of the behavior within the time period. This means that you should be in a position to observe the behavior clearly throughout the observation and be able to record the frequency of the behavior with limited distractions so that you do not miss an incident.

For instance, Sally took a frequency count of the number of requests Billy made during snack on Monday. The data indicated he made five requests, and the data collection period lasted 5 minutes. On Wednesday, Sally took another frequency count during snack – Billy made 10 requests during 10 minutes of data collection. If Sally just compares the frequency counts, it looks as though Billy's requesting was better on Wednesday than on Monday because the number of requests was higher. However, given that the duration of the times observed was different, this type of comparison is not a valid assessment of his performance.

Instead, Sally should use rate data. In rate data, Sally would divide the frequency counts by the time. So, with Monday's observation, she would divide five requests by 5 minutes for a rate of one request per minute. With Wednesday's data, she would divide 10 requests by 10 minutes for a rate of one request per minute. This would indicate that Billy's rate of requesting is identical over the two days and has not increased; instead he just had more time to make requests on Wednesday than on Monday.

Event-by-event recording. This type of data collection is often referred to as trial-by-trial data or trial-to-criterion data. Essentially, it is used to record responses to individual directions or problems.

Event-by-event recording is frequently used in discrete trials for teaching children with autism and other developmental disabilities. In discrete trials, traditionally, you would give an instruction and record all of the student's responses. So, if teaching imitation of hand clapping, you would say, "Do this" and clap your hands. You would then record if the child clapped his hands (a) independently, (b) needed a prompt to clap, or (c) did not engage in the behavior at all.

In addition to discrete trial uses by teachers, event-by-event recording is often used when a speech-language pathologist is working with a child on articulation skills for saying /s/, for example. The child is reading a story with frequent /s/ sounds, and the speech pathologist records each time the student says the sound correctly or says it incorrectly. Both of these examples of measurement yield a percentage of correct responses that can be measured against the criterion set for mastery for this student on this goal.

Event-by-event measurement allows you to assess accuracy or use of a skill in specific situations. For instance, it may be used to record a student's response to greetings while walking down the hall. Each event would be when a person greets the student and waits for a response. A + is recorded if he independently returns a greeting by saying "hi," a − is recorded if he does not respond, and a P is recorded if he needed a prompt to respond.

Discrete trial data sheet. This data sheet (see Figure 3.4) is useful for conducting discrete trial teaching programs that are delivered in a massed practice teaching format (i.e., presenting a series of the same skill for several trials consecutively) in individual or small-group instruction (Wolery, Bailey, & Sugai, 1988). The student's data is recorded in the triangles and graphed across the numbers in the middle of the form. This type of teaching lends itself well to teaching learning readiness skills such as following directions and imitating motor movements with objects, receptive language identification involving discrimination, and pre-academic skills like matching pictures or lowercase and capital letters. If you are teaching a larger group of students, a form like the embedded trial forms discussed later might be more advantageous.

The form provides the steps of the teaching program as well as space for recording the student's performance. This is helpful because it allows you to see the next step as you are working with the student. Another benefit of this form is that the data is self-graphing, eliminating the need for you to transfer the data to either a sheet of graph paper for graphing by hand or to enter the data into a spreadsheet to summarize the information and present it in a visual manner.

While the form provides a lot of information in one place for easy reference, it may be difficult to navigate for someone who is not familiar with it. To help, you can find a video (https://www.aapcpublishing.net/bookstore/books/9123.aspx) that shows how the data sheet is used as well as explicit instructions for the sections of the form and how to use it in Appendix A.

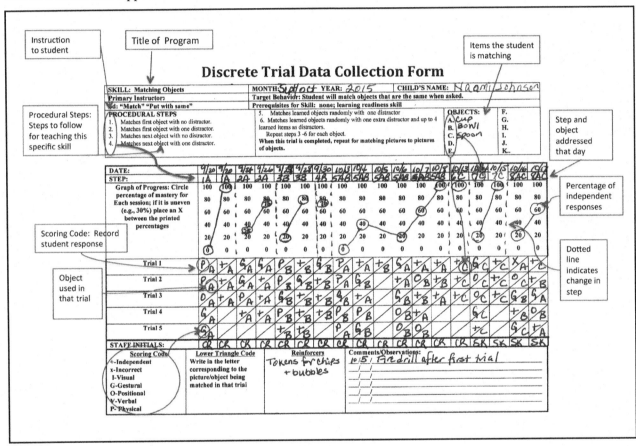

Figure 3.4. Discrete trial data sheet for teaching matching objects.

Mix-and-vary discrete trial data sheet. The data sheet in Figure 3.5 is useful when you are presenting discrete trials in a "distributed" fashion instead of the more traditional massed trial format. In distributed trials, a variety of skills are targeted and interspersed within each session (Wolery et al., 1988). For instance, the first trial might be to imitate clapping, the second to follow a direction for "touch nose," the third to identify a color, and the fourth to name a picture.

One advantage of this data sheet is that it can be printed on a 2-by-4 shipping label. (For easy portability, they can be put on a keychain as seen in Figure 1.15.). Each label provides a place to take data on a different skill while having all programs/targets the student is working on in one place, eliminating the need to flip through multiple data sheets during instruction. Using labels allows you to collect data over multiple days and then remove the labels for an individual skill and paste them in one place for consolidation and review of progress. For example, in the data sheet below, the discrimination label can easily be peeled from the data sheet and moved to a summary sheet of all the other sessions in which red/blue discrimination skills were taught.

The example shows the data on nine skills for one day: a color discrimination task using red and blue; labeling a pencil; naming body parts, including eye, ear, and nose; following one-step directions; preposition discrimination task using *under* and *on*; identifying a tool we eat with; identifying animals that have tails; labeling a fork; and stating last name. Note that over the course of instruction, the student receives between three and five trials for each skill, and the percent correct is based on independent performance only. Prompted trials are counted as incorrect. You can consolidate the labels for each skill and summarize the data by graphing it for analysis.

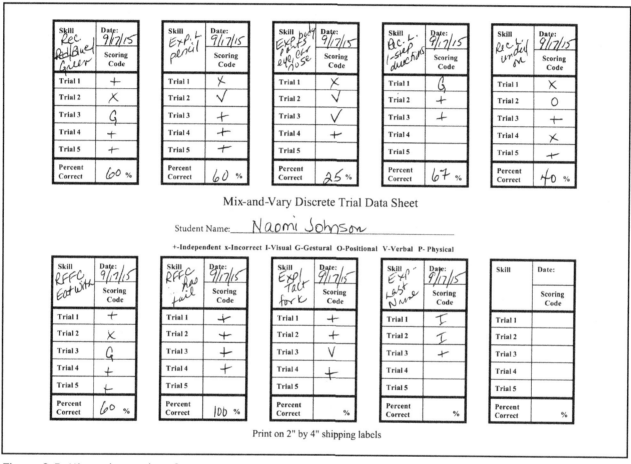

Figure 3.5. Mix-and-vary data forms.

Data Probes or Samples

Continuous data collection (taking data on each opportunity presented) provides you with more information for decision making than simply taking data on the first trial of each session (Cummings & Carr, 2009; Lerman, Dittinger, Fentress, & Lanagan, 2011). However, in some situations, it would be impossible to do so. For instance, if you were trying to track how many requests a student makes for desired items, you would have to count each request for that student throughout the entire day. Doing so while running a classroom and attending to other students would be difficult; besides, it is likely that the data will contain errors from times you could not observe him.

Some practitioners have addressed this issue by taking data on just the first opportunity to demonstrate the skill (sometimes referred to as cold probe data). Based on the limited research available, while this practice may provide a rough estimate of the student's progress, it may suggest that the student has mastered the skill sooner than he has and impact whether the skill is maintained over time (Cummings & Carr, 2009; Lerman et al., 2011).

Instead, Lerman and her colleagues (2011) recommend using continuous measurement when possible. Continuous measurement can be implemented with less difficulty when working 1-1 or in a very small group but would be difficult to implement when instructing students in more naturalistic situations. In order to address the need for continuous measurement of skills while reducing your data collection burden throughout the day, we often take samples of students' performance in specific activities. A data sample allows you to identify a specific activity or time period in which that skill is likely to occur and count in just that time period. Several samples taken throughout the week are often sufficient to provide data for problem solving and assessing the student's progress over time. Several data samples compared over time allow you to have an overall measure of the student's performance without tracking the skill all day of every day.

When taking data samples, it is important to use them consistently. Essentially, you want to ensure you are taking a sample for a specific period of time (e.g., the daily morning meeting that lasts 15 minutes). Specifying the start and stop time for the data collection is important for comparison purposes across days and weeks. You also want to ensure that data only includes performance demonstrated during that specific time period. For instance, you would not record a request that occurred on the playground on the data sample taken for morning meeting because this would contaminate the sample. Also, it is important to ensure that you are able to record and track every instance of the skill being assessed during the specified time period. Finally, it is helpful to take several data samples in different (2-3) activities over the course of a week. Not only does this make up for situations in which a student misses an activity, it also provides an assessment of the student's performance in different situations, which can be helpful in analyzing the data to problem solve if the student's performance is inconsistent. Samples are used most often in naturalistic situations when instruction is embedded within an ongoing activity. The following data sheets provide two formats for taking data samples over the course of a week, for either an individual student or a group of students.

Naturalistic sample data sheet for an individual. This data sheet is useful for collecting data on one student when the IEP objectives or curricular skills are embedded into several activities across the day (e.g., art, story time, fine motor) and you only need a sample of performance on the skill. We have used this data sheet frequently with students who are included for all or part of the day in a general education classroom and are supported by staff who are available to take the data. The sheet may also be used within a resource or self-contained classroom to track an individual student's progress across the day.

A major benefit of this tool is that the skills targeted are written under the activity during which they will be observed, which serves as a reminder for the classroom staff of the student's performance targets for each activity. The data is not self-graphing, so the student's progress must be summarized in another manner in order to make instructional decisions. Entering the data into a spreadsheet on a weekly basis and reviewing the resulting graphs will meet this need.

As illustrated in Figure 3.6, Angie is included for part of her school day in a kindergarten program with individualized support and part of the day in a resource classroom. The data sheet was used to track her skills on a weekly basis. Each day, the staff would take data on one row of the sheet, meaning they were tracking the frequency of one skill in each activity each day. Typically on Monday, they tracked the top row. So in direct instruction, they would take data on requesting help verbally when needed. On the day depicted, Angie needed help four times during direct instruction (typically these times were set up by her teacher), she made the request independently three times and needed a prompt for the fourth. In circle, they took data on raising her hand and waiting to be called on with a wait sign before making a request. She was independent at doing so twice but needed a prompt of some kind on two other occasions. In the play center, Angie independently requested items/actions using two- to three-word sentences twice and needed prompts two times. They continued to target following directions in art and raising her hand when requesting items in kindergarten.

On Tuesday, the teacher took data on requesting items missing or needed in direct instruction, and Angie was independent on two out of five opportunities. On following instructions given to a group, she was independent on three out of the five opportunities. She initiated play with a peer using language only two times during the play center on Tuesday. On Wednesday, they took data on the third row of skills, one skill in each activity. In the kindergarten block, Angie had the opportunity to follow instructions given to a group seven times, and the instructor (SM) just wrote the extra two responses above the five boxes.

Angie had a goal on her IEP for walking in line with her peers without touching those around her. This was something that only happened periodically during her day and would not produce enough opportunities to practice or take data to analyze if only taken one day per week. Consequently, the two boxes with darker shading and the direction "Check off daily" were included on the sheet, and each of the data boxes (those with + and P) represented one day and this data point was taken daily. This was conducted twice during her day to get two samples each day of her ability to walk independently in line without touching others.

Please note that there are five boxes under each skill. This is because we suggest that aiming for five opportunities for an activity provides enough data for analysis. As can be seen, more or less data can be recorded. Data on this sheet is taken in less detail than the data from the discrete trial data sheet because it is being taken within the context of larger activities, and typically the person taking the data is responsible for more than just taking data on this one skill. So, for the sake of accuracy, we reduced the amount of information collected. Finally, all the skills are being taught each day, but the data is only collected in samples. As illustrated, some of the skills repeated themselves, like maintaining a conversation for three turns. This allowed taking multiple samples during the week to both make comparisons and to accrue more information about Angie's performance.

Naturalistic Sample Data Sheet

Student: Angie Harding   **Teacher:** Sally McKenzie   **Week:** 9/26/15

Direct Instruction					Circle					Play					Art / Games					Kindergarten				
Request help verbally when needed					Raise her hand, wait to be called on with wait sign before making request					Request items/actions using a 2-3 word sentence					Follow directions from a peer in structured game					Raise her hand, wait to be called on with wait sign before making request				
+	p	+	+		+	+	p	p		+	+	p	p		+	+	+			p	p	+	+	p
Request items missing or needed					Follow instructions given to a group					Initiate play with a peer using language					Request items/actions using a 2-3 word sentence					Request help verbally when needed				
p	p	+	+	p	+	p	+	p	+	+	+				p	+	+	+		+	+			
Demonstrate consistent tripod grip when writing					Request desired items from peers					Look at her partner, wait for him to make eye contact, then make request					Request help verbally when needed					Follow instructions given to a group ++				
+	+				p	p	+	+		p	p	p	+		+	p	+	p	p	p	p	+	p	p
Maintain conversation for 3 turns					Maintain conversation for 3 turns					Request desired items from peers					Give and receive materials from peers independently					Maintain conversation for 3 turns				
+	p				p	+	p			+	p	+	+	+	+	p	+	p	+	+	+			
Walk in a line with peer without touching others (check off daily)					Request items/actions using a 2-3 word sentence					Ask for a turn when she wants to participate					Take turns with peer in a structure situation, give and receive materials					Walk in a line with peer without touching others (check off daily)				
p	+	X	p	+	+	p	+	p	+	+	+	p	+	p	+	+	+	+	+	+	p	+	+	+

+ = Independent P = Prompted X = Incorrect 0 = No Response; a blank means there was no opportunity to exhibit the skill

Figure 3.6. Naturalistic sample data sheet used for tracking one student's behavior.

Naturalistic sample data for a group. Although the data sheet shown in Figure 3.7 looks identical to the one shown in Figure 3.6, there is one major difference: It is used to collect data during one activity for multiple children. Some teachers find it is easier to have only one sheet of paper to manipulate during an activity. The downside to using this format is that the data must be summarized in some way, either by graphing by hand or by computer. Also, in order to store the data sheet in a child's folder, you need to delete the other children's data. One solution is to cut the data sheet into individual children's strips of skills and glue them onto a separate piece of paper. Another way is to set up the data sheet using address labels and peeling off an individual child's labels and sticking them onto a separate piece of paper.

Naturalistic Sample Data Sheet

Student: Morning Meeting **Teacher:** Sally McKenzie **Week:** 9/26/16

Sydney					Calen					Noni					Bill					Naomi				
Follows teacher directions to the group					Respond to greetings from adults					Recognizes her name by selecting it from field of 2					Recognizes picture by selecting from field 2					Recognizes picture by selecting from field 2				
+	+	x	p	+	p	p	O	p	+	+	+	+	p		+	+	+	+	+	p	p	p	+	p
Answers "What is it?" with a sentence					Requests a break					Follow a 1-step direction					Follow a 1-step direction					Answers a question in a 2-3 word sentence				
+	p	p	+	p	p	p	+	O		+	+	+	p	+	p	p	p	+	p	p	p	+	+	x
Identifies classmates by pointing or using their name					Identifies classmates by pointing or using their name					Requests a break					Responds to greeting from adult with gesture/vocalization					Follows 1-step direction				
p	p	p	X	p	+	p	p	X	p	+	+				+	+	+	p		+	+	p	p	X
Responds to greeting from adult verbally					Follows directions given to the group					Answers a question in 2-3 word sentence					Identifies classmates by pointing or using their name					Identifies classmates by pointing or using their name				
p	p	+	+		+	+	p	+	+	p	X	p	+	+	X	+	+	p	+	+	X	p	+	+

+ = Independent P = Prompted X = Incorrect 0 = No Response; a blank means there was no opportunity to exhibit the skill

Figure 3.7. Naturalistic sample data sheet — group.

In this data sheet, one of the aides takes the data during the group activity — one student's skills per day. So Sydney's data is taken one day, Calen's data is taken the next day, etc.

Checklist/task analysis data. Some skills taught within the classroom or community need to be broken down into component steps (task analysis) or an everyday classroom routine needs to be broken into a sequence of steps (functional routines), which are then taught and performed in a sequential order.

To take data on this type of skill, the steps for a task are typically laid out in the order in which the student must perform them. Using a data sheet for this kind of assessment, you would check off (a) the steps that the learner completes independently, (b) those he needs prompting for, and (c) those he does not complete. The steps stay constant with each observation and data are taken every time the skill is practiced or taken periodically as a sample. Typically this type of data yields a percentage of independent steps completed as a measurable number for comparison. For instance, Sarah independently completed 6 of 10 of the steps of the cleaning tables checklist, yielding 60% mastery of the steps.

Task analysis data sheet. The data sheet shown in Figure 3.8 allows you to note which of the steps the student is able to complete independently or needs a prompt to complete. It has the benefit of providing the staff with the instructional steps and data collection form in one place. It also has the advantage of self-graphing. The example is for a structured work system in which the student works independently to complete a series of mastered tasks.

STRUCTURED WORK TASK ANALYSIS DATA SHEET

SKILL: Work Basket System	WORKER'S NAME: Calen Barber
AREA: Cognitive/Learning	TARGET BEHAVIOR: Worker will complete a set of work baskets when given the Sd.
Sd: "Do your work", "work time" or "basket time"	PREREQUISITES: Worker can perform tasks in baskets independently.
PRIMARY INSTRUCTOR: Sally McKenzie	PROCEDURAL STEPS: Worker is prompted through basket activities with trainer using prompts. Prompts are gradually faded out.

DATE:	12/12/15	12/13/15	12/14/15	12/29/15	4/10/16	4/17/16	2/4/16	2/5/16
TIME:	10:15 AM	10:15 AM	10:15 AM	10:15	10:20	10:20	10:21	10:10
PROMPTS:	P, G	P, G	P, G	P, G	G	P, G	G	G
DURATION:	10m	9m	10m	10 M	11m	10m	9m	8m
BASKET ITEMS:	A B C	A B C	B A C	B C D	D A	B C	B D	A C D	D B C

Scoring Code:
/ Correct
- Prompted
X Incorrect
O Circle total correct

Prompts
P-Physical
G-Gestural
S-Visual
V-Verbal prompt from a distance
0-Does not perform step

Basket items steps (29 down to 1):
29. Occupies time appropriately after completing baskets.
28. Asks for help if materials are missing.
27. Accesses reinforcer.
26. Puts completed basket into "finished" basket or area.
25. Puts activity back into basket.
24. Completes activity.
23. Sets up activity.
22. Takes activity out of basket.
21. Places third basket in front of self.
20. Matches third shape.
19. Pulls off third shape.
18. Puts completed basket into "finished" basket or area.
17. Puts activity back into basket.
16. Completes activity.
15. Sets up activity.
14. Takes activity out of basket.
13. Places second basket in front of self.
12. Matches second shape.
11. Pulls off second shape.
10. Puts completed basket into "finished" basket or area.
9. Puts activity back into basket.
8. Completes activity.
7. Sets up activity.
6. Takes activity out of basket.
5. Places first basket in front of self.
4. Matches first shape.
3. Pulls off first shape.
2. Sits in chair.
1. Walks to basket area.

STAFF INITIALS: SM, SM, SM, SM, SM, SM, SM, SM

LEVEL OF MASTERY: 19/29/66%, 24/29 90%, 86%, 93%, 90%, 86%, 97%, 96%

Comments/Observations:
12/12/15 Needed help getting started

Criterion for Mastery: 100% for 3 weekly data samples

Basket Items: A. Put in Chips B. Pull Apart beads C. Transfer marbles D. Matching colors

Adapted from Nova Southeastern University Autism Program. Used with permission.

Figure 3.8. Independent work task analysis data sheet.

The data sheet in Figure 3.9 is for using a vending machine, a common life skill taught to secondary students on a functional curriculum because it is highly reinforcing. In this sheet, the data must be graphed after being collected, but it has the advantage of having the steps and directions written out for the staff in addition to the performance expected of the student.

Task Analysis Data Sheet With Method

Skill: Vending Machine	**Student's Name:** Sharon Kennedy
Area: Vocational	**Primary Instructor:** Jenny Davis
Direction: "Time to get a snack"	**Setting:** Cafeteria
Target Behavior: Makes a purchase from the vending machine	**Prerequisites:** Follow 1-step directions

	Date:	9/15/15	9/16/15	9/20/15					
Record the prompting level in each box.									
Step	**Method**								
Finds vending machine and stands in front of it	Say 'Let's go to the vending machine and get a: _____	+	+	+					
Identifies the item he needs on the machine	Point to item if needed	+	+	+					
Puts money in the machine	Give him the correct amount of money to insert in the machine	G	+	+					
Push correct button for item to purchase	Point if needed; block other options	+	+	+					
Gets the item from the machine	Use a point for a cue if needed	+	+	+					
Gets change from machine	Have him check for change even if had correct change	G	G	G					
Takes item to the person he bought it for	Use a verbal cue if needed to remind him who to take it back to	P	G	G					
	STAFF INITIALS:	JD	JD	JD					
	LEVEL OF MASTERY:	4/7	5/7	5/7					

Scoring Code:	**Comments/Observations:**
+-Correct X-Incorrect P-Physical V-Verbal prompt from a distance G-Gestural 0-Does not perform step S-Visual	___/___/_____ ___/___/_____ ___/___/_____
Criterion for Mastery: 7/7	**Materials:**

Adapted from Nova Southeastern University Autism Program. Used with permission.

Figure 3.9. This sheet tracks Sharon's progress on all the steps needed to make a purchase from a vending machine.

Other Types of Data Collection Tools for Quantified Performance Data

Toileting data sheet. It is important to take data when you are implementing a toileting program. Before beginning the program, it is helpful to track when the student urinates throughout the day, usually by doing a diaper check every half hour or noting when the student has a toileting accident. Once you have an idea of when the student urinates, you can schedule him or her to go to the bathroom to increase the likelihood of success. It is critical to track both the times the student actually uses the toilet, and when he does not. It is also important to track the times of the accidents so that you can see whether you are having any success. In Figure 3.10, Sydney was taken to the bathroom on a fairly consistent schedule during his day. He had two accidents during the time the data were reported and consistently urinated in the toilet when taken to the bathroom.

Toileting Data Sheet

Student's Name: Sydney Bell

Date	Time	U = Urinate B = Bm	Accident	Taken To Toilet	Self-Initiate
5/1/16	9:15		x		
5/1/16	11:15	U		x	
5/1/16	12:30	U		x	
5/1/16	1:45	--		x	
5/2/16	9:00	U		x	
5/2/16	11:15	U		x	
5/2/13	12:15	--		x	
5/2/16	2:00		x		
5/3/16	9:00	U		x	
5/3/16	11:00	U		x	
5/3/16	12:30	U		x	
5/6/16	Absent				
5/7/16	9:00	U		x	
5/7/16	11:00	U		x	
5/7/16	12:30	U		x	
5/7/16	1:45	U		x	

CODE: U-URINE B-BOWEL N-NOTHING

Figure 3.10. Toileting data sheet for Sydney.

Rubric for social interaction. The use of rubrics was discussed earlier in connection with work product or mastery level of an activity. Rubrics are also useful to measure acquisition of skills that do not result in a score but in an increase in the quality of the behavior. Social skills are an example of skills for which rubrics are appropriate to measure progress. For Susi, in Figure 3.11, several skills in the area of pragmatics were being targeted for improvement and needed monitoring to ensure the student was making progress. The data was taken when the student was on the playground with her peers.

Social Skills – Pragmatics Rubric
How Did I Do Today?

Name: Susi Shanholtz	Date: 9/18/15
Activity: Group work in English	Time: 9:15 a.m.
Rater: Sam Simpson	

For each skill, rate the student's behavior in the Score column with a 1, 2, or 3.

Skill	1	2	3	Score
Visually checks in with partner	Makes eye contact when listening to partner	Makes minimal eye contact when speaking to partner	Makes appropriate eye contact when speaking to partner	2
Stands at least 12-18 inches from partner	Stands 6 inches from partner	Stands 12 inches from partner	Stands 18 inches from partner	3
Matches facial expression to verbal message	Makes stated emotion on face in isolation	Has appropriate emotion on face in interaction 50% of time	Has appropriate emotion on face in interaction 80% of time	2
Shifts gaze to what partner is looking at or listening to	Shifts gaze to what partner is looking at/listening to in fleeting manner	Shifts gaze to what partner is looking at/listening to	Shifts gaze to what partner is looking at/listening to and rechecks with partner	1
Self monitors when vocal volume is too loud	Identifies when vocal volume is too loud for situation 50% of time	Identifies when vocal volume is too loud 90% of time	Regulates vocal volume when she sees she's too loud without adult prompt	2

Comments: This was a new group of students she hadn't worked with before, so she was a bit quieter than usual.

Figure 3.11. Social skills pragmatics rubric.

Travel card. At the secondary level, travel cards (originally designed by Laura Carpenter) are useful for students who move from class to class and from teacher to teacher. Such cards can be used to collect information on behavior, class participation, completion of assignments, and completion of homework, for example. Each teacher completes the information for her subject, and the card rotates through classes with the student. The information can be quantified by summing the number of pluses per week. In Figure 3.12, the teachers checked whether Corey's performance was attempted or performed as well as whether he exhibited anxiety during a given step. If anxiety was high, demands were adjusted.

Travel Card

Name: *Corey Trader*	Date: 9/24/15		
Raters: *Jenni Davis*	Notes:		
	Attempted	**Performed**	**Anxious**
Gym			
Engaged himself in appropriate activity	✓		
Responded to social initiation by peer	✓		
Initiated interaction with peer or adult		✓	✓
Stayed in gym for __20__ minutes	✓		
Cosmetology			
Engaged himself in appropriate activity		✓	
Responded to social initiation by peer		✓	
Initiated interaction with peer or adult	✓		
Stayed in cosmetology for __25__ minutes			
Woodworking			
Engaged himself in appropriate activity		✓	
Responded to social initiation by peer	✓	✓	✓
Initiated interaction with peer or adult		✓	
Stayed in woodworking for __40__ minutes	✓		
Agriculture			
Engaged himself in appropriate activity	✓		
Responded to social initiation by peer	✓		
Initiated interaction with peer or adult	✓		
Stayed in agriculture for __50__ minutes		✓	
Classroom			
Engaged himself in appropriate activity		✓	
Responded to social initiation by peer		✓	
Initiated interaction with peer or adult		✓	
Stayed in classroom for __50__ minutes		✓	✓
Other:_____			
Engaged himself in appropriate activity			
Responded to social initiation by peer			
Initiated interacted with peer or adult			
Stayed in classroom for _____ minutes			

Comments: *Classes are 50 minutes long today due to assembly*

Figure 3.12. Travel card.

Time-Based Recording

Duration data. Taking duration data (see Figure 3.13) involves recording the amount of time it takes a student to complete a task. For instance, a teacher could measure how long it takes a student to read a third-grade paragraph or how long it takes him to complete a structured work system. The teacher could also measure how long the student stays seated in a group activity or how long he works independently without prompting or asking for assistance.

Duration data is typically taken with a stopwatch or timer that can count up; the time starts when the direction is given and stops when the task is completed or when the student is no longer engaged in the task. This type of data can be useful for increasing time on task, increasing time working independently, or decreasing the amount of time it takes to complete a task.

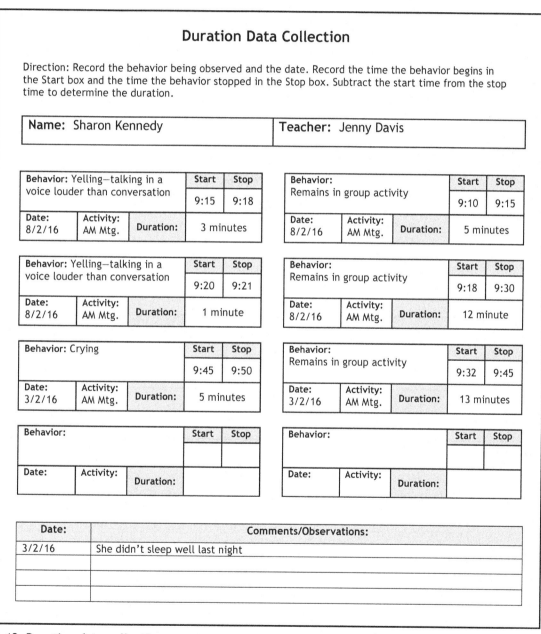

Duration Data Collection

Direction: Record the behavior being observed and the date. Record the time the behavior begins in the Start box and the time the behavior stopped in the Stop box. Subtract the start time from the stop time to determine the duration.

Name: Sharon Kennedy   **Teacher:** Jenny Davis

Behavior: Yelling—talking in a voice louder than conversation	Start	Stop
	9:15	9:18

Date: 8/2/16	Activity: AM Mtg.	Duration:	3 minutes

Behavior: Yelling—talking in a voice louder than conversation	Start	Stop
	9:20	9:21

Date: 8/2/16	Activity: AM Mtg.	Duration:	1 minute

Behavior: Crying	Start	Stop
	9:45	9:50

Date: 3/2/16	Activity: AM Mtg.	Duration:	5 minutes

Behavior:	Start	Stop

Date:	Activity:	Duration:	

Behavior: Remains in group activity	Start	Stop
	9:10	9:15

Date: 8/2/16	Activity: AM Mtg.	Duration:	5 minutes

Behavior: Remains in group activity	Start	Stop
	9:18	9:30

Date: 8/2/16	Activity: AM Mtg.	Duration:	12 minute

Behavior: Remains in group activity	Start	Stop
	9:32	9:45

Date: 3/2/16	Activity: AM Mtg.	Duration:	13 minutes

Behavior:	Start	Stop

Date:	Activity:	Duration:	

Date:	Comments/Observations:
3/2/16	She didn't sleep well last night

Figure 3.13. Duration data collection.
This data sheet was completed for Sharon to assess how long she remains in a group activity (as well as to track some challenging behaviors).

Latency data. When the question is how long it takes a student to start a task or to respond to a specific direction or communication, latency data is an appropriate measure. This type of data collection involves measuring the time between when a direction is given and when the student begins the task. Measuring the time between when the teacher says, "It's time to work" and when the student picks up his pencil and puts it on the paper is an example of latency. Similarly, with communication, latency data can be useful for measuring the amount of time it takes a student to respond to someone else's communication to him.

For instance, in Figure 3.14, the teacher, Sam, gave Josephine a direction, started the timer, and measured how long it took before Josephine began the task. Decreasing the latency of this time would indicate better attentiveness to the teacher. Typically, latency data is taken using a stopwatch and can easily be compared over time across similar skills.

Latency Data Collection

Directions: Record the date, activity, the direction that was given to the student (e.g., sit down, line up), and then the time the direction was given. Then record the time the student followed the direction. Subtract the time the direction was given from the time the student followed the direction to get the total time or latency.

Name: Josephine Baker   **Teacher:** Sam Simpson

Date	Activity	Direction Given	Time Direction Given	Time Student Started Following Direction	Total Time (Latency)	Prompts Provided
6/24/15	Reading seat work	Do page 24 in your workbook	10:05	10:08	3	
6/24/15	Math seat work	Do story problems 1-4 in your math book	11:40	11:45	5	Gestural

Date	Comments / Observations

Figure 3.14. Latency data collection.

The number of options for selecting useful and appropriate data collection forms for monitoring skill acquisition purposes is endless. To start, you need to have an idea of the type and amount of data that is necessary to document progress and problem solve when a learner has difficulty mastering a skill. Your selection of an appropriate form will help you "tame your data monster."

Chapter 4
Analyzing Skill Acquisition Data

Overview

Many types of data are collected on each student whose progress you are responsible for documenting. Some of the data is required by the school district or funding agency and is analyzed for you. Other data that you collect in your classroom or work environment you must analyze yourself to determine whether progress is being made or not and, based on the results, change your teaching procedures, materials, or setting, as needed to be more effective. This chapter will help you answer the following questions:

- Can you use a self-graphing data sheet that allows you to visually inspect the student's progress as you teach?

- What procedures or tools are available that will help you summarize data?

- How does technology help to analyze data for your use?

- What rules are available to make decisions about whether your teaching is effective?

State-Level Tests and Report Card Grades

Once you have selected forms and procedures for collecting data, you must determine how you are going to use the data to inform your instruction. Some of the forms that were presented in Chapter 3 are self-graphing and can be visually inspected to determine whether the student is making progress or not. Others require you to input the data into a spreadsheet to create graphs you can analyze. It is important that you have an idea of the rules for interpreting graphs that will help you adapt your instruction to ensure your students will be successful. These rules will be discussed in this chapter.

For students who are taught in general education settings, the yearly high-stakes testing, or end-of-course tests for high school students, serve as a summary measure of what students have mastered during the year. These scores allow for comparisons between an individual student's mastery of the curriculum and that of students across the state, school district, grade, and class.

Report card grades also serve as a summary measure and are typically made up of grades on homework assignments, classwork, and unit tests. Achievement can be compared to that of other students in the same class if accommodations and modifications are not considered in the grade. If they are, the student's mastery may be quite different from that of other students in the class.

These kinds of measures are not useful for making changes to a student's instructional program because the feedback does not occur frequently enough to know that a student is having difficulty mastering the curriculum or show the effects of changes to teaching techniques or other changes in the instructional environment. Consequently, you need more frequent data. Data systems that are designed to give frequent feedback make instruction more effective and efficient (Farlow & Snell, 1994).

For students who spend all or much of the day in general education settings but receive special education services, other types of data may be collected by the general education teacher, the special education teacher, or a paraprofessional. For example, work product labels (see Figure 1.9) may be used to document the amount of assistance the student needed to complete the assignment; tests or rubrics may be used to rate independence of performance or mastery of level of content (scores on the rubrics can be graphed to show progress over time).

For students who are educated in specialized settings and may be exempt from the state-mandated high-stakes tests, other summary assessments are used. Currently, they differ from state to state. Some states use tests based on established access points or alternate standards based on a modified curriculum with accommodations to the way the test is administered. Other states use portfolios of documented student work and teacher-collected data to ensure that students are making progress over the course of the year. Portfolios may be in alignment with students' IEP goals/objectives or measure other defined access point skills based on the state-established alternate curriculum. It is difficult in such cases to make comparisons to other students' achievement, but these types of data do provide a summary measure of the student's growth on mastery of the year's content.

Report card grades for students on alternate standards being educated in special education classrooms are often more difficult to interpret due to varying practices across districts. Most districts grade students on their achievement with accommodations and modifications provided, but do not provide information about how the student accomplished the mastery. As a result, one student could receive an "A" in reading, while reading three grade levels below grade assignment, with maximum teacher cueing. Another student may receive an "A" in reading, while reading four grade levels below grade assignment, independently.

Therefore, while there are systems in place for measuring progress to report to state and local agencies comparing students' performance to established standards, this type of data is taken and reported on a periodic basis (e.g., each nine weeks, yearly). Information that requires you to wait for a minimum of nine weeks before analyzing whether the student is successfully mastering content could result in the student falling farther behind. In addition, the time lag before making changes to a teaching program that is not working may result in students making errors in learning that then have to be corrected, resulting in more lost time.

Curriculum-Based Assessments

When students are being educated using commercially available alternate curricula, it is important to take advantage of the curriculum-based assessments that typically come with the product. For example, when the Strategies for Teaching Based on Autism Research (STAR; Arick, Loos, Falco, & Krug, 2004) program is used with young children, the assessment is completed three times a year, and the mastery of skills in various domains can be graphed to visually represent the progress. By administering the assessment at the beginning of the year, after the winter break, and again at the end of the year, you may also obtain information that would help to make extended school year (ESY) decisions. For example, if your student had mastered matching picture to picture prior to winter break but does not do so when he returns from break, you would monitor to determine how long it takes for him to regain the skill. Delays in recoupment of the skill would be one indication that the student needs ESY services. The same type of decision-making process could be used with similar curricula like the Brigance Comprehensive Inventory for Basic Skills-II (Curriculum Associates, 2010), the Verbal Behavior Milestones Assessment Protocol (VB-MAPP; Sundberg, 2008), or the Assessment of Basic Language and Learning Skills-Revised (ABLLS-R; Partington, 2006). An alternate curriculum that is correlated with the Common Core Standards is the

ULS (https://www.n2y.com/products/unique). The ULS provides checkpoints that serve as pre- and post-assessments for the monthly units taught to provide an ongoing assessment of the skills being addressed, as illustrated in the following example.

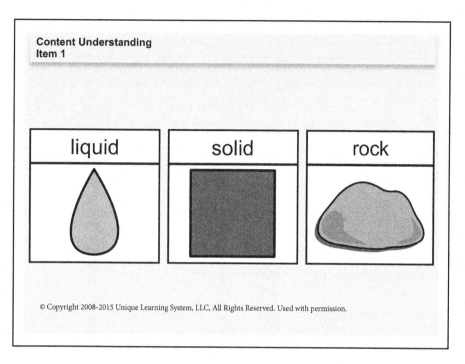

Figure 4.1. A screenshot from the ULS monthly checkpoint for assessing progress within the curriculum.
NOTE: The directions to the student are "Marshall has a red baloon. It is filled with water. What is water?" To respond, the student touches the correct picture of "liquid" on the screen or with the picture cards.

The checkpoints can be administered via computer or tablet or can be printed and presented by the teacher. There are standard instructions on how to implement the assessments and they can be given monthly or at the end of each thematic unit in the curriculum.

Data Sheets

Collecting frequent data allows the teacher and other classroom staff to evaluate whether the student is mastering a skill or is having difficulty mastering it. Several of the data sheets that have been presented in this book are self-graphing, making it easy to see the progress, or lack of progress, such as the event-by-event data sheet and the task analysis/functional routines data sheet shown in Figure 4.2. This data sheet allows the teacher to take data on each of the steps of completing a structured work system and then graph the progress across the days by circling the number of steps completed independently, circling that number and connecting the lines across the days.

STRUCTURED WORK TASK ANALYSIS DATA SHEET

SKILL: Work Basket System	**WORKER'S NAME:** Calen Barber
AREA: Cognitive/Learning	**TARGET BEHAVIOR:** Worker will complete a set of work baskets when given the Sd.
Sd: "Do your work", "work time" or "basket time"	**PREREQUISITES:** Worker can perform tasks in baskets independently.
PRIMARY INSTRUCTOR: Sally McKenzie	**PROCEDURAL STEPS:** Worker is prompted through basket activities with trainer using prompts. Prompts are gradually faded out.

DATE:	12/12/15	12/13/15	12/14/15	12/29/15	1/10/16	1/17/16	1/24/16	2/5/16
TIME:	10:15 Am	10:15 AM	10:15 Am	10:15	10:20	10:20	10:21	10:10
PROMPTS:	P,G	P,G	P,G	P,G	G	P,G	G	G
DURATION:	10m	9m	10m	10 M	11m	10M	9m	8M
BASKET ITEMS:	A B	C A	B C	B A	C B	C D D A	B C	B D D B	C
29. Occupies time appropriately after completing baskets.	29	29	29	29	29	29	29	29
28. Asks for help if materials are missing.	28	28	N/A	N/A	28	N/A	28	28
27. Accesses reinforcer.	27	27	27	27	27	27	27	27
26. Puts completed basket into "finished" basket or area.	26	26	26	26	26	26	26	26
25. Puts activity back into basket.	25	25	25	25	25	25	25	25
24. Completes activity.	24	24	24	24	24	24	24	24
23. Sets up activity.	23	23	23	23	23	23	23	23
22. Takes activity out of basket.	22	22	22	22	22	22	22	22
21. Places third basket in front of self.	21	21	21	21	21	21	21	21
20. Matches third shape.	20	20	20	20	20	20	20	20
19. Pulls off third shape.	19	19	19	19	19	19	19	19
18. Puts completed basket into "finished" basket or area.	18	18	18	18	18	18	18	18
17. Puts activity back into basket.	17	17	17	17	17	17	17	17
16. Completes activity.	16	16	16	16	16	16	16	16
15. Sets up activity.	15	15	15	15	15	15	15	15
14. Takes activity out of basket.	14	14	14	14	14	14	14	14
13. Places second basket in front of self.	13	13	13	13	13	13	13	13
12. Matches second shape.	12	12	12	12	12	12	12	12
11. Pulls off second shape.	11	11	11	11	11	11	11	11
10. Puts completed basket into "finished" basket or area.	10	10	10	10	10	10	10	X
9. Puts activity back into basket.	9	8	9	9	9	9	9	9
8. Completes activity.	8	8	8	8	8	8	8	8
7. Sets up activity.	7	7	7	7	7	7	7	7
6. Takes activity out of basket.	6	6	6	6	6	6	6	6
5. Places first basket in front of self.	5	5	5	5	5	5	5	5
4. Matches first shape.	4	4	4	4	4	4	4	4
3. Pulls off first shape.	3	3	3	3	3	3	3	3
2. Sits in chair.	2	2	2	2	2	2	2	2
1. Walks to basket area.	1	1	1	1	1	1	1	1
STAFF INITIALS:	SM	SM	SM	SM	SM	SM	SM	SM
LEVEL OF MASTERY:	19/29/66%	26/29 90%	86%	93%	90%	86%	97%	96%

Scoring Code:	Prompts	Comments/Observations:
/ Correct	P-Physical	12/12/15 Needed help getting started
- Prompted	G-Gestural	/ /
X Incorrect	S-Visual	/ /
O Circle total correct	V-Verbal prompt from a distance	
	0-Does not perform step	

Criterion for Mastery: 100% for 3 weekly data samples	Basket Items: A. Put in Chips B. Pull Apart beads C. Transfer materials	D. Matching E. colors F.	H. G. I.	I. J. K.
		G.	K.	L.

Figure 4.2. Independent work task analysis data sheet.

Other skill acquisition data sheets, including the embedded trials sheet and the group data collection sheet, require the information be transferred to a spreadsheet to be graphed. A graphing template that covers a school year is available for downloading at https://www.aapcpublishing.net/bookstore/books/9123.aspx and is discussed later in the chapter.

Graphing Data

Research clearly shows that the students of teachers who graph their data and review the graphs on a regular basis (e.g., weekly) make more progress (Fuchs & Fuchs, 1986). In general, research recommends reviewing data on a student's progress at least every two weeks with at least five new data points collected (Browder & Spooner, 2011; Farlow & Snell, 1994) so that a trend line can be developed. If the data sheet does not provide this display as part of the data collection, the teacher must develop a system for summarizing the data to graph it.

Data can be graphed using paper and pencil or a variety of technology. Some teachers prefer to graph the data by hand. Others prefer to use a spreadsheet program like Excel or Google Drive. As noted above, some of the data sheets allow you to graph the data as you take it on the sheet itself. Regardless of the way that data are graphed, here are some helpful guidelines.

1. Develop graphs in a consistent manner with fixed X- and Y-axes. This allows them to be compared over time and to each other. Typically, the top of the Y-axis is the highest data point possible. Hence, if a teacher is graphing performance by percent of correct responses, the highest Y data point would be 100%. Setting the Y-axis lower than this would lead the observer to think that more progress is being made than is actually the case. In the example in Figure 4.3, the student's performance is exactly the same, but because the data on the right rise farther in relation to the Y-axis, it looks as though the student is making more progress. Consequently, consistency in graphing is key to accurate interpretation (Farlow & Snell, 1994).

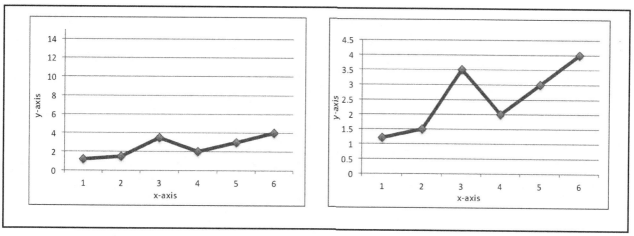

Figure 4.3. A comparison of two graphs of the same data with different Y-axes.

2. Choose a graphing form that can be used throughout the semester. Decide whether to include five days per week or seven days per week on the graph. We find it best to use a seven-day-a-week graph so that weekend days are shown as blanks. This makes it possible to see if there is a pattern to the data when the student is away from school. This type of interpretation can help in making ESY determinations, for example. Using a format in which the data can be graphed on the same graph throughout the semester allows you to draw aim lines that indicate the level of mastery when it is predicted in the IEP. For instance, if you are starting school in September and an objective or benchmark is to be mastered at 80% by the end of the second quarter, a dot can be drawn where mastery is expected and a line drawn from current performance to the mastery goal to develop an aim line. The aim line then becomes the mechanism for comparing performance to determine if the goal or objective will be met on time. This helps when reporting progress when the categories reported are mastery and progressing toward mastery versus not expected to master the goal (Browder & Spooner, 2011; Farlow & Snell, 1994). An example is shown in Figure 4.4.

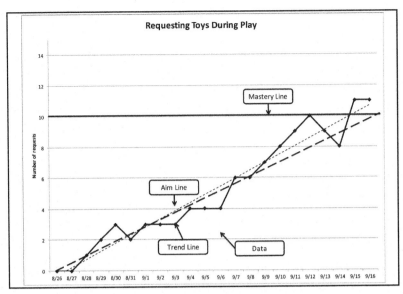

Figure 4.4. Graph of the number of requests with the aim line parallel to the trend, showing on-time mastery.

3. Add data to graphs at least weekly as data points are collected so that they can be reviewed. The authors have found it useful to schedule data review sessions into teachers' weekly routine of meetings. Administrators who set aside time for teachers to review their data, often with the educational team, are putting a priority on the collection and use of data in making decisions throughout the school. Because data analysis is often a single-person pursuit – usually left up to the teacher or the therapist – it is rarely included in the overall plan for preparatory activities in the staff's week.

At one school for children with special needs, we were able to set aside Thursday afternoons after school as the time for data to be summarized and reviewed. No meetings were scheduled on Thursdays in the building, and the expectation was that this time was for teachers and therapists to summarize and review their data. This program had the opportunity to include paraprofessionals in this collaboration, which helped them to understand how the data they collected was used to determine students' progress. While this type of collaboration is rarely available in school systems because paraprofessionals leave when the students leave, it continues to be important to ensure that the information is shared with them. In this program, "Data Thursday" helped to keep the data from piling up and becoming a significant burden on the teachers and, ultimately, improved instructional decisions.

We suggest that even if a school does not adopt this practice, teachers and therapists schedule a regular time within their week to summarize the data. Without explicitly setting a time in the planner to do this, the data tends to pile up. The more data there is to summarize, the less motivated a person is to gather the data and work on it, and the harder it is to start the process.

4. Connect data points across the graph for consecutive days of data collected, but do not connect data points for nonconsecutive days (Farlow & Snell, 1994). In Figure 4.5 there was a three-day weekend. Consequently, data was not collected over the weekend (2/20, 2/21) or on the Monday holiday (2/22). Data was collected again on Tuesday. The data points for the previous week, Monday to Friday, were connected by a solid line, but the line would not connect Friday to Tuesday since data was not collected.

This makes it easy to see when data is missing (for whatever reason) and helps interpret changes in the data in relation to when the skill was taught or data was collected.

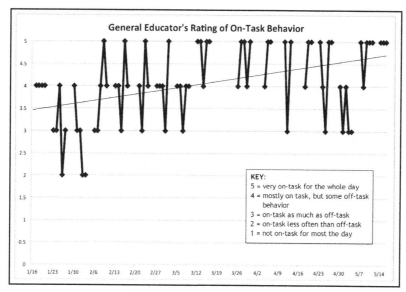

Figure 4.5. Rating of on-task behavior demonstrating gaps of missing data days (e.g., weekends, holidays).

5. Use dotted or solid vertical lines to represent phase changes or changes to the program or circumstances in any significant way. Mark these so you remember what they are and, therefore, are able to analyze their effects. Do not connect data points across these lines. This helps to decrease the time it takes to determine what the progress on the graph means because changes to the program are visually clear (Farlow & Snell, 1994).

Traditionally, solid vertical lines represent major changes in a program such as changes from baseline data collection (no intervention) to implementation of instruction or a change in the intervention strategy. Dotted lines are used to indicate minor changes to the program like a shift in reinforcement or a new step within the same teaching program as seen in Figure 4.6 (Cooper et al., 2007).

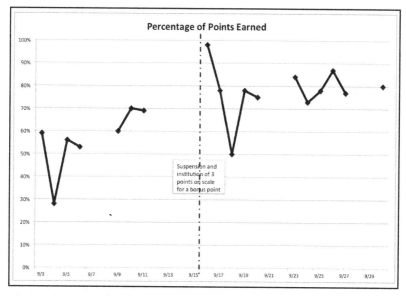

Figure 4.6. Graph depicting the use of a phase line (dotted line) to indicate a change in the behavior point system being recorded.

Graphing template. To assist teachers in regular graphing of ongoing data on skills they teach, we have developed a graphing template for Excel™ from Microsoft Office. You can download a copy of the spreadsheet at this link: https://www.aapcpublishing.net/bookstore/books/9123.aspx.

This template (shown in Figure 4.7) allows you to enter data for each week across a variety of activities. It was initially designed to be used with the naturalistic sample data sheet (see Figures 3.6 and 3.7), with the data collected in several activities at least once a week. The graph is updated each year with new weekly dates. It is set up so that data from three activities can be totaled across the week. You put in the number of unprompted responses and the number of total opportunities for each activity. Across the line, if you delete the extra #N/A for any cells that are not used for data, the data across activities will total and determine the percent of trials that were completed independently. The data from the spreadsheet will then transfer to the graph. On weeks for which there is no data, delete the #N/A across the week. They will then show up as gaps on the graph to indicate that data was not taken (e.g., over the winter break) and allow for assessing regression/recoupment discussions for extended school year decisions. (See video of the graphing process: https://www.youtube.com/watch?v=Wb-MXT9Tjt4/.)

Goal/Obj	Activity 1			Activity2			Activity3			Total			
Week	Ind.	Opp.	Percent	Ind.	Opp.	Percent	Ind.	Opp.	Percent	Ind.	Opp.	Percent	
11/29/2010		#N/A	#N/A		#N/A	#N/A		#N/A	#N/A	0	#N/A	#N/A	
12/6/2010		#N/A	#N/A		#N/A	#N/A		#N/A	#N/A	0	#N/A	#N/A	
12/13/2010		#N/A	#N/A		#N/A	#N/A		#N/A	#N/A	0	#N/A	#N/A	
12/20/2010		#N/A	#N/A		#N/A	#N/A		#N/A	#N/A	0	#N/A	#N/A	If the program hasn't started yet, leave the #N/A and don't delete the rows.
12/27/2010		#N/A	#N/A		#N/A	#N/A		#N/A	#N/A	0	#N/A	#N/A	
1/3/2011		#N/A	#N/A		#N/A	#N/A		#N/A	#N/A	0	#N/A	#N/A	
1/10/2011		#N/A	#N/A		#N/A	#N/A		#N/A	#N/A	0	#N/A	#N/A	
1/17/2011	2	4	0.5	0	2	0				2	6	0.33333	
1/24/2011													
1/31/2011	5	5	1	0	3	0	3	3	1	8	11	0.72727	
2/7/2011	5	5	1							5	5	1	
2/14/2011	3	4	0.75				0	3	0	3	7	0.42857	
2/21/2011													If there was school and data just wasn't collected (e.g., student absent), delete all the text from that week.
2/28/2011	3	4	0.75	0	2	0				3	6	0.5	
3/7/2011	3	5	0.6	0	2	0	0	3	0	3	10	0.3	
3/14/2011													
3/21/2011				2	2	1				2	2	1	
3/28/2011													
4/4/2011													
4/11/2011	4	4	1				3	3	1	7	7	1	
4/18/2011		#N/A	#N/A		#N/A	#N/A		#N/A	#N/A	0	#N/A	#N/A	For future dates, leave the #N/A in place to prevent it from graphing 0s.
4/25/2011		#N/A	#N/A		#N/A	#N/A		#N/A	#N/A	0	#N/A	#N/A	
5/2/2011		#N/A	#N/A		#N/A	#N/A		#N/A	#N/A	0	#N/A	#N/A	
5/9/2011		#N/A	#N/A		#N/A	#N/A		#N/A	#N/A	0	#N/A	#N/A	
5/16/2011		#N/A	#N/A		#N/A	#N/A		#N/A	#N/A	0	#N/A	#N/A	

Figure 4.7. Graphing template that allows you to enter data from naturalistic data samples and automatically graphs the data.

Data Analysis

Once your data has been graphed, it is time to analyze it to see whether the student is making adequate progress or whether changes need be made to the instructional program. There are many reasons why the student may not be making adequate progress (e.g., the reinforcer is not powerful enough or delivered frequently enough, the connection between the delivery of the reinforcement and the performance of the skill is not clear, the steps to the instructional program are too large and need to be broken down, or the student needs some 1:1 instruction instead of small group). The following are guidelines for interpreting the data.

1. Review data weekly when you have at least three to five new points to evaluate (Farlow & Snell, 1994). This can be done as part of the graphing procedures discussed above. Again, it is important to schedule it into the weekly routine of the classroom.

2. Compare the trend of the data to the aim line for the skill. Determine if the performance is exceeding the aim line, following the aim line, or falling below the aim line. A graph depicting the use of an aim line can be seen in Figure 4.8. If the data is exceeding or following the aim line, then continue the program as it is. If the data is falling below the aim line, problem solving is needed to determine how to address the problem. To make this analysis, you need to be able to review at least five to six data points. If such data are not available, more data are needed (Farlow & Snell, 1994). For these situations, you will need to adopt a problem-solving strategy to help interpret the data to make changes to the student's program. Using a problem-solving system results in better interpretation of the data as well as better student performance (Browder & Spooner, 2011; Farlow & Snell, 1994).

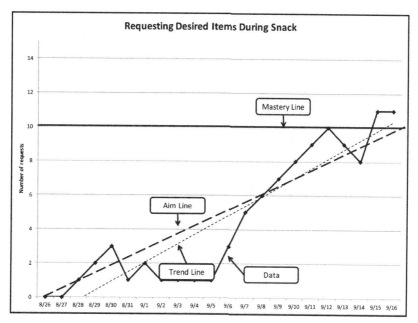

Figure 4.8. Trend line (dotted line) and mastery line (solid line) to aid in determining potential for mastery.

In Figure 4.8, the straight dotted diagonal line is a trend line. In the Excel spreadsheet available online, you can select the data series and right click your mouse. This will produce a menu that includes "Trend line." By clicking this, the program will draw a trend line on the data to use for comparison. (Please note that at the time of this publication, other software such as Google Drive's spreadsheet does not support this feature.) When the trend line is drawn, you can determine if it shows that the skill is increasing, decreasing, or staying flat. Skills that are increasing are making progress. Compare them to the aim line to determine if it is enough progress to meet the goal. Trends that are decreasing may be an indication that a student's performance is getting worse and should be evaluated (see Troubleshooting Instructional Problems below). Trends that are flat indicate that the student's performance has plateaued. Consequently, it is time to change something about the instruction (e.g., the routine, the teaching program, the reinforcers) to get the performance moving again.

3. Evaluate the variability of the data. Variability refers to the scatter of the data points over time (Cooper et al., 2007; Wolery et al., 1988). Data with low variability or low scatter is typically reliable for decision-making. Highly variable data, as shown below, makes it difficult to determine progress and indicates scattered performance from day to day. This may reflect inconsistent or unreliable data collection, unreliable student performance, or an insufficient number of opportunities to get a good sense of the student's true performance.

In Figure 4.9, the student demonstrated 0% performance on some days and 100% on others. This may mean that the student's performance varied significantly from day to day due to behavioral or motivation issues. It may also mean that there were few opportunities to practice the skill. For instance, if only one opportunity was given per day and the student was successful, his performance was 100%. If he did not respond, his performance would be 0%. Cases of high variability must be analyzed for potential problems with performance as well as data collection and instruction (Farlow & Snell, 1994; Wolery et al., 1988).

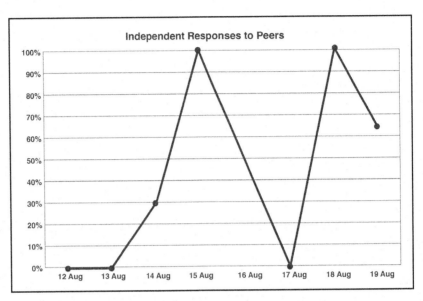

Figure 4.9. Significant variability in the data may indicate potential problems with instruction as well as performance.

4. Look at the level of the data. The level of the data indicates whether the student's performance is high or low (Farlow & Snell, 1994; Wolery et al., 1988). For instance, data with a level trend at a high level may indicate mastery of the skill. Data with a flat trend at a low level may indicate that the skill is too difficult, as shown in Figure 4.10.

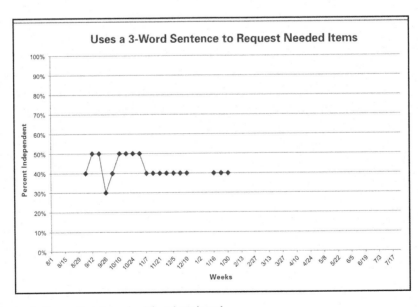

Figure 4.10. Graph depicting a flat trend with a low level.

Troubleshooting Instructional Problems

If the aim line and the trend line of the graphed data indicate that the student is not making progress, the team needs to look at the qualities of the data on the graph to decide what action to take. Research indicates that teachers who used a decision-making system increased the accuracy of their decisions about data (Haring, Liberty, & White, 1980; Jimenez et al., 2012).

Data-based decision system. Several systems may be used to evaluate data. Browder and her colleagues (Browder & Spooner, 2011) have developed an empirical decision system for evaluating data. The system is summarized below as it was used (with a slight change in order) in the latest research by Jimenez and colleagues (Jimenez et al., 2012).

TABLE 4.1

Data-Based Decision System for Students With Severe Disabilities

Data Pattern	Change Needed	Examples of Options
Mastery	Introduce new skills	Introduce new science terms Target a new daily living skill
Adequate Progress	Make no changes	
Slow Progress	Improve antecedents	Use time delay to fade prompts Use/fade stimulus cues
Inconsistent Progress	Improve motivation	Vary reinforcers Offer choice of materials Have student self-monitor
No Progress	Simplify/shape responding	Use assistive technology Teach a subset of the skill

Mastery is indicated when the trend is increasing and the level is high or the trend has plateaued but the level is high and in the range of mastery. When this pattern is observed, it is time to introduce a new skill or a new step in the program (Browder & Spooner, 2011; Jimenez et al., 2012). This might mean moving on to the next step or moving on to the next skill if the mastery level and all the targets are met in the current program. For instance, it may include adding more vocabulary words to the receptive identification program or adding the learned vocabulary words from the receptive program to the expressive program. Clearly this level is the desired end goal.

Adequate progress is met when the trend line of the data indicates the data are climbing up the aim line and the goal is likely to be mastered when projected to do so. Typically, this involves an increasing trend with little variability or scatter in the data points (Jimenez et al., 2012). Adequate progress is illustrated in Figure 4.11.

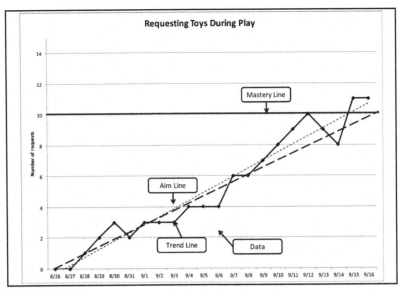

Figure 4.11. Graph depicting adequate progress being made with a steady upward trend.

Slow progress is demonstrated in Figure 4.12, in which the data trend line is moving up the aim line but, if it continues at this rate, it is unlikely to reach mastery at the projected date. In this case, you can see the dotted line, which is the aim line, indicating the path of progress needed to master the goal, while the solid diagonal line is the trend line representing the path of the actual data.

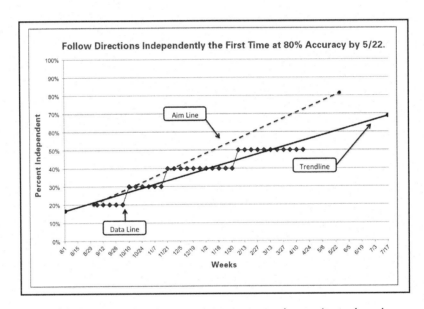

Figure 4.12. Graph depicting slow or inadequate progress to meet the projected goal.

Typically, this indicates a need to improve antecedents, such as changing the prompting strategy. Sometimes slow progress is an indication that staff are jumping in too soon or too often with prompting and need to fade cues more effectively (Jimenez et al., 2012). Slow progress may also mean that you need to change the size of the steps in the teaching. For instance, if you are shaping increased time spent in a group activity, and the steps you are using are too large (e.g., 10 minutes, 20 minutes, 30 minutes), it may take the student longer to make progress. Since he is getting reinforced less frequently, smaller jumps in time are required. He may progress more quickly if the time segments being shaped are reduced (e.g., 2 minutes, 5 minutes, 8 minutes) so that he is reinforced for meeting the criteria more frequently.

Inconsistent progress, or data with high variability, like the example in Figure 4.13, can indicate a variety of issues.

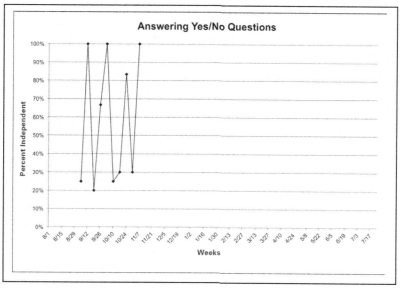

Figure 4.13. Graph depicting inconsistent progress.

The following are some examples of interpretations of inconsistent progress.

- There have been insufficient numbers of opportunities, as discussed above, which lead to an all-or-nothing pattern of data (e.g., %0 and 100% are commonly seen next to each other).

- The value of the reinforcers is variable so that the responding is inconsistent. A solution would be more frequent changing of the reinforcers to avoid satiation or reassessing to find new reinforcers that might be more effective (Cooper et al., 2007; Farlow & Snell, 1994; Jimenez et al., 2012).

- There is a problem with student compliance. This might be addressed by changing the instruction to make it more engaging, mixing up tasks to maintain engagement, offering a choice of activities, or having the student self-monitor (Cooper et al., 2007; Farlow & Snell, 1994; Jimenez et al., 2012).

- There is a need to return to teaching some basic learning readiness skills such as sitting quietly and following directions. A student who has difficulty with basic learning readiness skills is likely to demonstrate erratic performance due to missing the instruction because he or she was not attending.

- For students with ASD and similar learning difficulties, their highly variable performance might be due to sensory interference or behavioral or physical issues that should be addressed.

- Data may vary based on who is taking the data. Differences in the observation and recording of the data on the behavior may lead to variations in the data that have little to do with instruction or the student's performance. Instead they result because the definition of the skill is not clear to the observers and they are actually recording different behaviors. This is a sign that the teacher needs to review the definitions of the target skill and ensure that all staff recording data have a clear understanding of what they are observing and recording.

No progress, like that shown in Figure 4.14, is typically reflected in a low level with a flat trend and little variability (Wolery et al., 1988). It usually indicates that the student has not moved forward. It presents a good reason for regular analysis of the data to avoid this discovery nine weeks rather than nine days into the teaching process. These data point to a need to simplify the tasks presented, break the task into smaller steps, go back to an easier or a foundational skill and reteach. For instance, if a learner is not making progress using a picture schedule independently and has not shown any ability to be independent on the steps, you may want to assess if the learner can match the pictures on the schedule. Without this foundational skill, the student cannot be expected to make progress with a picture schedule but may need an object schedule instead.

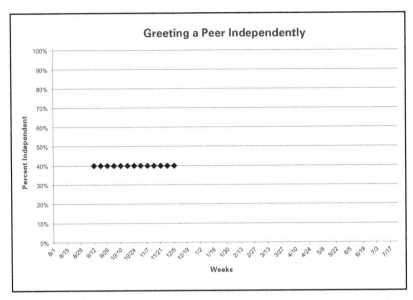

Figure 4.14. Graph depicting no progress is being made.

Problem analysis worksheet. Teachers may find it helpful to analyze the data with more information than just the line on the graph by using the Problem Analysis Worksheet (Figure 4.15; Farlow & Snell, 1994, p. 17). Using the worksheet in Figure 4.15, you graph the data and evaluate the trend, variability, and level, as described above. You then review the data graph and check off the characteristic that applies (e.g., the data is not variable) or indicate if you "Need More Data" (NMD) to make a decision. The checklist goes on to ask questions about medication schedules, temporary factors such as environmental changes, and possible problems with data reliability. It then analyzes the trend and variability to see if it has changed since the last review, whether the variability appears randomly, or whether it is cyclical.

Variability or trends that have changed since the last review may indicate that something in the student's life or daily routine has changed and has impacted the skill acquisition or that the student has hit a part of the teaching program that is difficult for him. One example is a student who is making good progress on identification of pictures when they are presented alone, but has difficulty and progresses more slowly when having to discriminate those pictures from each other. It might also indicate that instruction has changed from a 1:1 to a 1:2 staff-to-student ratio or that the schedule has changed and the skill is being taught at a different time or in a different place.

Next, you must determine whether the variability is random or has a pattern. Variability with a pattern may indicate outside factors are at play, such as different performance with different instructors. For example, random variability may indicate some internal factor such as illness is playing a role. Cyclical variability may indicate a pattern related to medication or physical illnesses or to something external that is cycled as a change; for instance, if the staff changes once a month so the student is working on the skill with a different teacher each month. Another variable is to assess if there is a difference between test data (no help given) and teaching data each month (prompting provided) to see if the student performs differently under those different conditions.

Another area of the worksheet assesses the type of errors the student makes. If the errors seem to be on the same step, it would indicate a need to address problems within that specific step (e.g., break it down into smaller steps). If the student is not showing progress in the fading of prompt levels, perhaps prompting procedures need to be evaluated or reinforcement to be increased for reducing prompting from physical to gestural prompting rather than only when the skill is independent.

It is also important to review patterns of errors to see if they occur more frequently at the beginning or end of the teaching session. Errors that occur at the beginning of the session might indicate a need for instruction of easy tasks at the beginning to get the student engaged in instruction. Errors that occur primarily at the end of the session might indicate that the student is losing engagement as the session progresses and that, therefore, teaching may need more variability or teaching sessions may need to be shorter.

Finally, the worksheet asks questions to determine if errors are setting- or staff-specific. For instance, does the student not attend to the task or the cues? If so, those elements may need to be changed to make them more engaging. Is the student receiving reinforcement for incorrect performance? If so, the staff needs more training on implementing error correction procedures and reinforcement use. Are noncompliant and interfering behaviors present? If behaviors are interfering with instruction, then a functional behavior assessment may be needed to address them before progress can be made.

PROBLEM ANALYSIS WORKSHEET

Put a check (✓) by the statements which you feel describe the data collected during the latest review period.
Circle NMD if you suspect the statement describes the data, but you Need More Data to answer the question.

1.	The trend of the data is:	ascending	.... 1.	❏	NMD
		flat	....	❏	NMD
		descending	....	❏	NMD
2.	The data are:	not variable	.... 2.	❏	NMD
		variable	....	❏	NMD
3.	The level of the data is:	low	.... 3.	❏	NMD
		moderate	....	❏	NMD
		high	....	❏	NMD

4. Student performance is related to medication schedules. .... 4. ❏ NMD
5. Student has experienced a temporary environmental change/problem/stress. .... 5. ❏ NMD
6. The data may not be reliable. .... 6. ❏ NMD
7. The staff are not implementing the program reliably. .... 7. ❏ NMD
8. The trend or level of variability has changed since the last review. .... 8. ❏ NMD
9. The student used to perform the skill at higher levels. .... 9. ❏ NMD
10. The data pattern indicates that variability is random. .... 10. ❏ NMD
11. The data pattern indicates that variability is cyclical. .... 11. ❏ NMD
12. Test data conflict with the instructional data. .... 12. ❏ NMD
13. Test scores tend to be greater than instructional scores. .... 13. ❏ NMD
14. Errors typically occur on the same step(s) of the task analysis. .... 14. ❏ NMD
15. The student is not showing progress on prompt levels. .... 15. ❏ NMD
16. Errors typically occur on the first trials of the day or session. .... 16. ❏ NMD
17. Errors typically occur on the latter trials of the day or session. .... 17. ❏ NMD
18. Errors are setting or staff specific. .... 18. ❏ NMD
19. The student does not attempt the task. .... 19. ❏ NMD
20. The student does not attend to the cues .... 20. ❏ NMD
21. The student is receiving reinforcement for incorrect performance. .... 21. ❏ NMD
22. The student exhibits similar problems in other programs. .... 22. ❏ NMD
23. The student is noncompliant with the programs. .... 23. ❏ NMD
24. Interfering behaviors are present. .... 24. ❏ NMD
25. Problem behaviors are staying the same or increasing. .... 25. ❏ NMD
26. The program does not facilitate student access to interaction with peers. .... 26. ❏ NMD

State your hypotheses about the instructional problems based on the above information.

_____

_____

_____

_____

From Farlow and Snell (1994). Used with permission from American Association on Intellectual and Developmental Disabilities (AAIDD).

Figure 4.15. Problem analysis worksheet.

As illustrated, the problem analysis worksheet essentially takes you through the problem-solving process of looking at the data to evaluate all the elements that may play a role in the student's performance. From the answers to the questions, you can form a hypothesis about the problems with the data and how to address them.

The example in Figure 4.16 analyzes the graph from Figure 4.10 focusing on a student whose data had leveled off after she initially was making progress. After reviewing the various options, it became clear that the staff were giving her items she needed when she used one or two words, rather than prompting her, waiting, and reinforcing with the needed item when she used a three-word sentence. Hence the student showed progress in some situations but not in others. This discovery indicated to the teacher that she had to do some retraining of the rest of the staff about how to teach the skill.

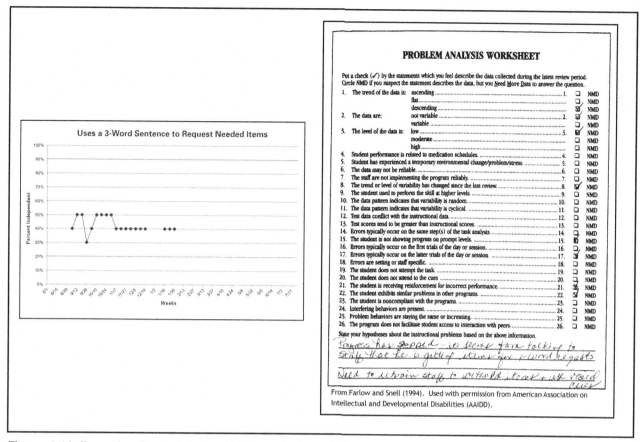

Figure 4.16. Example of completed problem analysis worksheet.

Chapter 5
Data Collection for Measuring Challenging Behavior

Overview

Many elements of challenging behavior may need to be measured when a student is exhibiting behavior problems. This chapter will help you select the appropriate measures to determine the function(s) of behavior and to measure the effectiveness of a behavior plan.

- How do you choose the correct data collection instrument for the behavior you are measuring?

- Do you have the resources in your environment to collect data on the behavior of concern (i.e., staff skill, time)?

- What instruments are available to help you collect data on challenging behavior (e.g., timers, counters)?

- What technology is available to measure targeted behavior?

Challenging behaviors present themselves in many different ways and, therefore, require different measures. This chapter provides information about the types of data collection forms and systems that can be used to measure frequency, rate, duration, and intensity.

Challenging behavior can be addressed programmatically in several ways. One way is to address a challenge in the classroom before it reaches the level of significance needed for more formal assessment. This type of initial strategy is used frequently in RTI programs as a Tier 1 or 2 intervention in schools as well as by instructors addressing behaviors that are interfering with learning in any setting. Another way is to develop an IEP goal with benchmarks or objectives to increase an appropriate behavior. This typically occurs when challenging behaviors are interfering regularly with instruction and less formal measures are not effective. A third approach is to complete a functional behavior assessment (FBA) that attempts to determine the purpose or underlying motivation of the problem behavior and how it responds to factors in the environment. From the FBA, the instructor develops a behavior intervention plan (BIP), and data is then collected to monitor the effectiveness of the plan.

While the first two methods of addressing challenging behavior focus primarily on measuring the occurrence of the targeted behaviors, the FBA process not only monitors the occurrence but also requires collection of additional data to determine the relationship between the targeted behavior and events in the environment. Both types of data collection needs are addressed in this chapter.

Defining the Target Behavior

Your first step in developing data collection systems for challenging behavior is to develop a clear definition of the specific behaviors you wish to decrease. Defining the behaviors to be decreased is critical to deciding what type of data collection is needed. Well-defined target behaviors include objective information about what exactly is observed when the behavior occurs. For instance, a good definition would describe the observable characteristics of the behavior, as opposed to being emotional or interpreting the behavior. That is, in order to measure behavior, the observer has to be able to see the behavior and know it has occurred (Cooper et al., 2007). For instance, rather than "John became angry," an observable statement might be "John began to strike others around him with an open palm."

Target behaviors must also be clear and unambiguous so that everyone collecting the data will record the same behavior, resulting in reliable data (Cooper et al., 2007). Therefore, the behavior might be defined for this student as "hitting includes making physical contact with another person's body in a way that makes an audible sound to the observer."

Finally, the definition should be complete so that observers know when to start counting a behavior and when to stop (Cooper et al., 2007). For a student who engages in whining, the definition might be: "whining involves making repeated statements with a high-pitched tone of voice or in a sing-song manner. When whining begins, the stopwatch will be started to count the occurrence. If the whining stops for more than 3 seconds, the stopwatch will be stopped, and a new occurrence of the behavior will begin when the whining begins again."

Dimensions of Behavior for Measurement

Once you have a clear definition of the target behavior, you can determine the type of data you need to assess it. Three dimensions in the assessment and monitoring of challenging behavior are frequency (how often they occur), duration (how long they last), and intensity (how severe they are). (Table 5.1 depicts the types of behavior that lend themselves to different types of data collection.)

A key element in determining the type of information you need is whether the behavior is brief (i.e., it begins and ends quickly and can be easily counted) or extended in its presentation (i.e., it lasts for more than a minute). Brief behaviors are better measured with frequency whereas those that last longer are best measured using duration. Similarly, for behaviors that occur occasionally, frequency or rate data are good choices, whereas behaviors that happen too frequently to get an accurate count may be measured using a sampling procedure. When it seems that there is a pattern to the behavior in terms of time of day, particular subject matter being taught or activities occurring, or person interacting with the student when the behavior occurs, it may help to develop a scatterplot that counts the occurrences of behavior occurring under each of the conditions. Each type of data will be addressed within this chapter.

TABLE 5.1
Matching Data Collection to Type of Behavior

Behavior	Type of Data Collection
Aggression involving specific events such as hitting, kicking, and biting	Frequency or rate and/or intensity rating scale
Self-injurious behaviors involving specific events such as hitting self, hitting body part against something else, self-biting	Frequency or rate data and intensity data. A time sampling procedure could be used if the behavior is so frequent that frequency is likely to be inaccurate; however, the risks of the time sampling for such a significant behavior has to be considered
Tantrum, crying, screaming, or other behaviors that involve longer periods of time engaged in the behavior	Duration, partial interval or momentary time sampling, and/or intensity, rating scale
Stereotypical behavior such as flapping, rocking	Partial interval, momentary time sampling, rating scale, or duration
When it seems that there is a pattern to when a behavior occurs (e.g., time of day, subject matter being taught, adult who is working with the student)	Scatterplot

Behaviors that are brief, lasting only a few seconds, and occur only occasionally may be counted using frequency or rate measures. If occurring repeatedly or many times throughout the day, these same behaviors may not be counted accurately using a frequency count. For instance, Jim's hitting happens frequently throughout the day and in order to track it with a frequency count, the teacher would have to be sure Jim was always within his sight. This isn't practical while trying to run a classroom, so the teacher took a sample of his behavior by taking a frequency count in three different 20-minute periods throughout the day, each day. This gave him a sample that he could then extrapolate to a rate for the day and compare over time.

For behaviors that are longer lasting and diffuse (e.g., crying, tantrum, stereotypical behavior), taking a frequency count would not necessarily yield changes in data if the dimension that changed was how long they lasted. For instance, two 3-minute tantrums might be considered better than one 20-minute tantrum, despite the decrease in frequency. For those behaviors, duration becomes the important element to assess. At times, however, behaviors last too long or happen too frequently to accurately assess by taking the duration of each episode. For those behaviors, a time sampling procedure such as partial interval or momentary time sampling data might give an estimate of the significance of the problem. If time sampling is not a possibility in the setting for staffing or activity reasons, a rating scale might be used to give an estimate of the seriousness of the problem for that period of the day using a numerical rating scale with behaviorally defined anchors like the one in Figure 5.1. Anchors serve as guidelines to the raters to increase the consistency across different observers.

| 5 = very on task for the whole activity |
| 4 = mostly on task, but some off-task behavior |
| 3 = on task as much as off task |
| 2 = on task less often than off task |
| 1 = not on task for most of the activity |

Figure 5.1. Example of anchors for a rating scale assessing on-task behavior.

Finally, for some behaviors, the primary element of concern is how intense or severe the behavior is. For instance, sometimes when John hits other students, it is simply a tap; at other times, he punches them with a closed fist. For these types of behaviors, a scale that is created with anchors like Figure 5.2 may be a way to assess whether the behaviors are more or less severe over time.

1	2	3	4	5
No behavior Incidents	Some whining, crying, pushing	Moderate; some hitting, crying, yelling	Biting, scratching for periods of time	Urinating, biting, scratching, inconsolable

Figure 5.2. Example of anchors for rating scale assessing overall challenging intensity.

Types of Data Collection for Challenging Behavior

Frequency data. When it is important to know how often a behavior is occurring, frequency data is taken. You might use frequency data for informal assessments for challenging behaviors interfering with learning (such as in RTI) and for monitoring goals/objectives in the individual's learning program or a behavior intervention plan. As seen in Chapter 3, this is a very common measurement that simply counts the number of occurrences of the behavior. Examples of frequency data include the number of times a child hits a peer; the number of times a child falls to the floor, kicking and screaming; and the number of times a student runs out the door during instruction. If the only challenging behaviors being tracked are of such intensity that they result in an incident report, referral to the office, and/or suspension, then these reports can also provide some measure of frequency data. Care should be taken, however, that these are collected consistently to provide a reliable measure.

The data sheet shown in Figure 5.3 allows you to take data on the frequency of several behaviors at the same time over a one-month period. You fill in the code or color the square, starting from the bottom of the sheet, each time the targeted behavior occurs. Space at the bottom allows you to write in different behaviors with different codes if you need to differentiate the forms of behavior that are occurring (e.g., throwing, hitting). The data then form a graph of the behavior for the month.

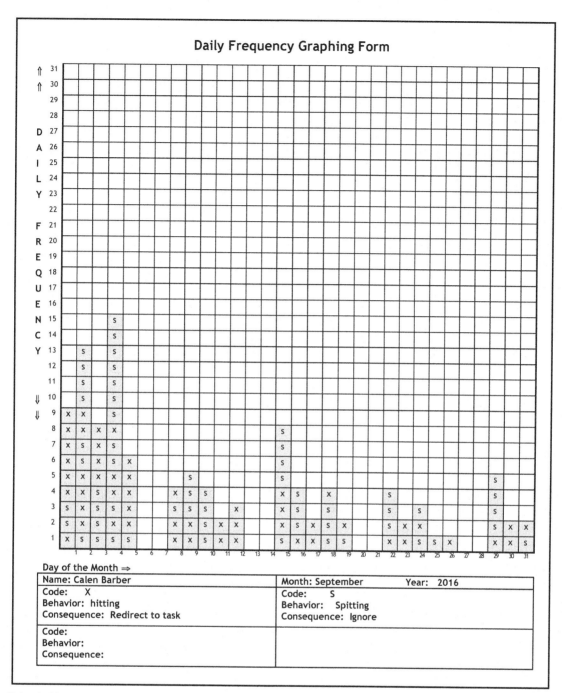

Figure 5.3. Self-graphing frequency data sheet.

Rate data. As described in Chapter 3, rate data is simply frequency data taken within a set amount of time. Rate data allows for comparison of the frequency of behavior when the data is taken for different periods of time. In order to take rate data, you must first take frequency data while tracking the amount of time being observed as well. The rate of a child hitting a peer might be obtained by counting the number of times the child hits a peer in a 15-minute period; or the number of times a child has a tantrum, as defined above, in a 6-hour school day; or the number of times a student runs out of the classroom during instruction over a school week. For example, Bill exhibited five instances of challenging behavior during a 6-hour day on the first of the month. This can be calculated to show a rate of behavior of .83 incidents per hour.

Duration. Sometimes it is important to know how long a behavior lasts, because the behavioral change is targeting an increase or decrease in time during which a behavior is occurring. This would be the case in increasing the amount of time a child is attending to a group activity, sitting in a chair, or engaging with a particular toy. You might also use duration to assess a behavior that lasts longer than a few seconds (e.g., crying). Behaviors targeted for decreasing duration may include length of a tantrum or length of a crying episode for a child who is having difficulty separating from his parent when he begins preschool.

When you are tracking the duration of a behavior, it is important to have access to a clock with a second hand or a stopwatch/timer that counts up in order to get an accurate measure of the duration of the behavioral incident. Examples of data sheets for tracking duration are presented in Figures 5.4 and 5.5. In Figure 5.4, Sharon's behaviors are being tracked to analyze the amount of time she spends yelling and crying and the amount of time she participates in a group activity. With this form, the teacher can track both positive and negative behaviors at the same time. Duration data was chosen because the team could count the number of instances from the duration data sheet and still analyze whether Sharon was spending more time in group activities and less time engaged in challenging behavior over time, which gave them a better assessment of the improvement of the behavior than just a frequency count.

In Figure 5.5, Bill in Sally's class shows that he was screaming for a total of 50 minutes during this one day. Each sheet is used to record minute-by-minute duration of a specific behavior. It is easy to use because it just involves shading the times he was screaming.

Duration Data Collection

Direction: Record the behavior being observed and the date. Record the time the behavior begins in the Start box and the time the behavior stopped in the Stop box. Subtract the start time from the stop time to determine the duration.

Name: Sharon Kennedy	Teacher: Jenny Davis

Behavior	Start	Stop	Date	Activity	Duration
Yelling—talking in a voice louder than conversation	9:15	9:18	8/2/16	AM Mtg.	3 minutes
Remains in group activity	9:10	9:15	8/2/16	AM Mtg.	5 minutes
Yelling—talking in a voice louder than conversation	9:20	9:21	8/2/16	AM Mtg.	1 minute
Remains in group activity	9:18	9:30	8/2/16	AM Mtg.	12 minute
Crying	9:45	9:50	3/2/16	AM Mtg.	5 minutes
Remains in group activity	9:32	9:45	3/2/16	AM Mtg.	13 minutes

Date:	Comments/Observations:
3/2/16	She didn't sleep well last night

Figure 5.4. Duration data collection.

Minute-by-Minute Duration Data

Directions: X or shade in each minute that a target behavior is occurring. Write the duration for each 30-minute segment at the bottom of the column.

Name: Bill Madison	Date: 8/10/16
Target Behavior: Screaming	Teacher: Sally McKenzie

7:00	7:30	8:00	8:30	9:00	9:30	10:00	10:30	11:00	11:30	12:00	12:30	1:00	1:30	2:00	2:30	3:00	3:30
7:01	7:31	8:01	8:31	9:01	9:31	10:01	10:31	11:01	11:31	12:01	12:31	1:01	1:31	2:01	2:31	3:01	3:31
7:02	7:32	8:02	8:32	9:02	9:32	10:02	10:32	11:02	11:32	12:02	12:32	1:02	1:32	2:02	2:32	3:02	3:32
7:03	7:33	8:03	8:33	9:03	9:33	10:03	10:33	11:03	11:33	12:03	12:33	1:03	1:33	2:03	2:33	3:03	3:33
7:04	7:34	8:04	8:34	9:04	9:34	10:04	10:34	11:04	11:34	12:04	12:34	1:04	1:34	2:04	2:34	3:04	3:34
7:05	7:35	8:05	8:35	9:05	9:35	10:05	10:35	11:05	11:35	12:05	12:35	1:05	1:35	2:05	2:35	3:05	3:35
7:06	7:36	8:06	8:36	9:06	9:36	10:06	10:36	11:06	11:36	12:06	12:36	1:06	1:36	2:06	2:36	3:06	3:36
7:07	7:37	8:07	8:37	9:07	9:37	10:07	10:37	11:07	11:37	12:07	12:37	1:07	1:37	2:07	2:37	3:07	3:37
7:08	7:38	8:08	8:38	9:08	9:38	10:08	10:38	11:08	11:38	12:08	12:38	1:08	1:38	2:08	2:38	3:08	3:38
7:09	7:39	8:09	8:39	9:09	9:39	10:09	10:39	11:09	11:39	12:09	12:39	1:09	1:39	2:09	2:39	3:09	3:39
7:10	7:40	8:10	8:40	9:10	9:40	10:10	10:40	11:10	11:40	12:10	12:40	1:10	1:40	2:10	2:40	3:10	3:40
7:11	7:41	8:11	8:41	9:11	9:41	10:11	10:41	11:11	11:41	12:11	12:41	1:11	1:41	2:11	2:41	3:11	3:41
7:12	7:42	8:12	8:42	9:12	9:42	10:12	10:42	11:12	11:42	12:12	12:42	1:12	1:42	2:12	2:42	3:12	3:42
7:13	7:43	8:13	8:43	9:13	9:43	10:13	10:43	11:13	11:43	12:13	12:43	1:13	1:43	2:13	2:43	3:13	3:43
7:14	7:44	8:14	8:44	9:14	9:44	10:14	10:44	11:14	11:44	12:14	12:44	1:14	1:44	2:14	2:44	3:14	3:44
7:15	7:45	8:15	8:45	9:15	9:45	10:15	10:45	11:15	11:45	12:15	12:45	1:15	1:45	2:15	2:45	3:15	3:45
7:16	7:46	8:16	8:46	9:16	9:46	10:16	10:46	11:16	11:46	12:16	12:46	1:16	1:46	2:16	2:46	3:16	3:46
7:17	7:47	8:17	8:47	9:17	9:47	10:17	10:47	11:17	11:47	12:17	12:47	1:17	1:47	2:17	2:47	3:17	3:47
7:18	7:48	8:18	8:48	9:18	9:48	10:18	10:48	11:18	11:48	12:18	12:48	1:18	1:48	2:18	2:48	3:18	3:48
7:19	7:49	8:19	8:49	9:19	9:49	10:19	10:49	11:19	11:49	12:19	12:49	1:19	1:49	2:19	2:49	3:19	3:49
7:20	7:50	8:20	8:50	9:20	9:50	10:20	10:50	11:20	11:50	12:20	12:50	1:20	1:50	2:20	2:50	3:20	3:50
7:21	7:51	8:21	8:51	9:21	9:51	10:21	10:51	11:21	11:51	12:21	12:51	1:21	1:51	2:21	2:51	3:21	3:51
7:22	7:52	8:22	8:52	9:22	9:52	10:22	10:52	11:22	11:52	12:22	12:52	1:22	1:52	2:22	2:52	3:22	3:52
7:23	7:53	8:23	8:53	9:23	9:53	10:23	10:53	11:23	11:53	12:23	12:53	1:23	1:53	2:23	2:53	3:23	3:53
7:24	7:54	8:24	8:54	9:24	9:54	10:24	10:54	11:24	11:54	12:24	12:54	1:24	1:54	2:24	2:54	3:24	3:54
7:25	7:55	8:25	8:55	9:25	9:55	10:25	10:55	11:25	11:55	12:25	12:55	1:25	1:55	2:25	2:55	3:25	3:55
7:26	7:56	8:26	8:56	9:26	9:56	10:26	10:56	11:26	11:56	12:26	12:56	1:26	1:56	2:26	2:56	3:26	3:56
7:27	7:57	8:27	8:57	9:27	9:57	10:27	10:57	11:27	11:57	12:27	12:57	1:27	1:57	2:27	2:57	3:27	3:57
7:28	7:58	8:28	8:58	9:28	9:58	10:28	10:58	11:28	11:58	12:28	12:58	1:28	1:58	2:28	2:58	3:28	3:58
7:29	7:59	8:29	8:59	9:29	9:59	10:29	10:59	11:29	11:59	12:29	12:59	1:29	1:59	2:29	2:59	3:29	3:59
6	2	0	5	4	0	8	3	2	0	5	3	5	0	3	2	2	N/A

TOTAL DURATION: 50 minutes

Comments/Observations

__/__/__ ______________________________

__/__/__ ______________________________

__/__/__ ______________________________

__/__/__ ______________________________

__/__/__ ______________________________

Adapted from www.behaviordoctor.com. Used with permission.

Figure 5.5. Minute-by-minute duration data sheet.

Time sampling. There are several procedures for taking data on behaviors that occur at such a high frequency that it is unlikely that classroom staff would be available to count them throughout the day. In that case, you are really taking a sample of the behavior based on intervals (i.e., specified time periods) of the day. However, it is important to be consistent about which format you are using: partial interval when you count the behavior if it occurred at any time during the interval, or momentary time sampling when you count the behavior if it was occurring at the end of the specified time period.

Partial interval time sampling. When behaviors occur at a high frequency or rate, it is often impossible for you to take accurate data while at the same time instructing the class or managing the learner. In those cases, you might use a specific type of interval recording called partial interval time sampling. In this type of data collection, the period of time during which data will be taken in the course of the day is defined and broken into smaller periods of time. For example, a teacher may break a 6-hour school day into 15-minute intervals so there would be 24 periods of data collection during the day. Partial interval time sampling counts whether the targeted behavior has occurred at any time during each of the 15-minute periods. It does not matter how long the behavior lasted or how many times the behavior happened during that interval. This is usually reported as a percentage of the number of intervals in which the behavior occurred.

The time frame should be broken down into segments that are small enough to capture an incident of the targeted behavior. If you are able to focus your attention on the learner without any other activities (e.g., without teaching other students at that time), the intervals can be smaller. If you are monitoring a group of students or have other activities to attend to, you should choose a larger interval. This helps to ensure that you can be accurate in the observations. For instance, if you made the interval 15 seconds but missed a 15-second period because you were distracted by someone else in the room, then the data would not be reliable. One of the advantages of partial interval data is that once the behavior occurs for the interval, you will no longer have to attend until the next interval begins because you are only recording whether at least a single instance of the targeted behavior occurs during that interval. For example, if you are taking data with 15-minute intervals and the student gets out of his seat (i.e., the target behavior) during the second minute, you can attend to other learners or other tasks until the next 15-minute interval begins. Partial interval time sampling typically overestimates the frequency of behavior, so it is best used for behaviors targeted to decrease because it may indicate a higher level of behavior than is being exhibited (Cooper et al., 2007).

Figure 5.6 provides an example. Here, the day is broken down into 10-minute intervals and covers a 1-week period. The target behavior is described, and the individual responsible for collecting the data checks off whether it occurred at any time during the 10-minute interval. The total number of intervals in which the behavior occurred is then counted, and a percentage of the total number of intervals during the day that the behavior occurred is computed. The shaded areas indicate time periods before or beyond the school day. A time when Phillip was late to school is also shaded to provide information about why the behavior did not occur during that time. It could also have been coded as behavior not occurring with an explanation under Comments at the bottom.

Interval Data Collection

Directions: Circle the type of interval data being collected. Put a tally mark or X in the interval if a target behavior occurred during that time period.

Name: *Phillip Masters*	Teacher: *Jenny Davis*
Target Behavior: *Putting hand in mouth*	Type of Data Collection: (Partial) Momentary Whole

Date →	8/25/16	8/26/16	8/27/16	8/28/16	8/29/16
7:00-7:10					
7:10-7:20					
7:20-7:30					
7:30-7:40					
7:40-7:50					
7:50-8:00					
8:00-8:10	X				
8:10-8:20	X			X	
8:20-8:30	X			X	
8:30-8:40			X		X
8:40-8:50	X				X
8:50-9:00	X				X
9:00-9:10	X				X
9:10-9:20	X	X			
9:20-9:30				X	
9:30-9:40				X	
9:40-9:50			X	X	X
9:50-10:00	X				X
10:00-10:10	X	X	X		X
10:10-10:20	X	X			
10:20-10:30	X				
10:30-10:40	X				
10:40-10:50					
10:50-11:00	X		X	X	
11:00-11:10	X		X		
11:10-11:20					X
11:20-11:30		X			
11:30-11:40		X		X	
11:40-11:50		X			
11:50-12:00				X	
12:00-12:10					
12:10-12:20			X		X
12:20-12:30		X			
12:30-12:40		X			
TOTAL	14	8	6	8	9
PERCENT					

Date →	8/25/16	8/26/16	8/27/16	8/28/16	8/29/16
12:40-12:50	X		X		
12:50-1:00	X	X		X	
1:00-1:10	X		X		
1:10-1:20				X	
1:20-1:30		X			
1:30-1:40			X		
1:40-1:50	X				X
1:50-2:00	X	X			X
2:00-2:10	X		X		
2:10-2:20	X	X			
2:20-2:30		X	X		
2:30-2:40					
2:40-2:50					
2:50-3:00					
3:00-3:10					
3:10-3:20					
3:20-3:30					
3:30-3:40					
3:40-3:50					
3:50—4:00					
TOTAL	7	5	4	3	2
PERCENT	54	37	26	28	28

Date	Comments / Observations
8/25/16	*School hours 8-2:30*
8/26/16	*Late to school*

Figure 5.6. 10-minute partial interval data sheet.

Momentary time sampling. A second type of data collection that is useful for high-frequency behaviors is momentary time sampling. In this type of procedure, you record whether the targeted behavior occurs at the end of the defined time interval. As with partial interval data, the recorder uses set time intervals and at the end of each interval, records whether the target behavior was occurring at that time. It is reported in the same way as partial interval time sampling, as a percentage of intervals in which the behavior occurred.

An advantage of momentary time sampling is that you only have to attend to the child exhibiting the behavior at the end of the defined period and can carry out other classroom duties during the rest of the time. Typically, you can use a vibrating timer or a smartphone with an interval app (e.g., D.A.T.A. app from behaviorscience.org) in your pocket to cue you to check the behavior. We will discuss the use of apps in Chapter 7. To record the momentary interval data, you can use the same data sheet that was used for partial interval data in Figure 5.6. In the example in Figure 5.7, the teacher marked off any interval during which the behavior was occurring at the end of the interval, 15 minutes in this case. The end of the day is shaded to show that Susi was not in school at that time.

The number of segments of the day in which the behavior occurred are added up, and the percentage of intervals in which the behavior occurred is computed by dividing number of intervals by total intervals during the day and multiplying by 100 (i.e., on 9/25/16, Susi was out of her seat at the end of 31% (or 8) of the intervals).

Interval Data Collection

Directions: Circle the type of interval data you are collecting under Type of Data Collection. Put a tally mark or X in the interval if a target behavior occurred during that time period.

Name: *Susi Shanholtz*					Teacher: *Sam Simpson*				
Target Behavior: *Out of assigned area at the end of the 15—minute period*					Type of Data Collection: Partial (Momentary) Whole				

Date →	9/25/16	9/26/16	9/27/16	9/28/16	9/29/16	10/2/16	10/3/16	10/4/16	10/5/16	10/6/16
7:30-7:45		X					X	X	X	
7:45-8:00				X		X				X
8:00-8:15					X	X	X			
8:15-8:30	X		X						X	X
8:30-8:45					X		X	X		
8:45-9:00	X					X				
9:00-9:15				X						
9:15-9:30		X								
9:30-9:45						X			X	X
9:45-10:00	X				X			X		
10:00-10:15		X								
10:15-10:30				X		X	X			X
10:30-10:45		X	X							
10:45-11:00	X				X	X			X	
11:00-11:15		X						X		
11:15-11:30	X		X			X				
11:30-11:45										
11:45-12:00			X	X			X		X	X
12:00-12:15										
12:15-12:30								X		
12:30-12:45		X		X	X	X				
12:45-1:00										
1:00-1:15	X			X			X		X	
1:15-1:30	X	X			X					
1:30-1:45			X					X		
1:45-2:00	X					X				
2:00-2:15										
2:15-2:30										
2:30-2:45										
2:45-3:00										
3:00-3:15										
3:15-3:30										
3:30-3:45										
3:45-4:00										
TOTAL	8	7	5	6	6	9	6	6	6	5
PERCENT	31%	27%	19%	23%	23%	35%	23%	23%	23%	19%

Date	Comments / Observations

Figure 5.7. Interval data sheet used for momentary time sampling.

Intensity

Another facet of behavior that may need to be measured to determine whether the behavior is getting better or not is the intensity, or magnitude, of the behavior. For example, for one person "hitting" may be a strong tap on the arm, while for another it may be severe enough to cause a person to recoil or cause the person pain. One way to track intensity is to develop a rating scale with definitions for each point along the scale, as illustrated in the following examples.

Calendar rating. In Figure 5.8, at the end of the school day, the teacher assigned a number (from 1-5) to the behaviors for the day and recorded it on a calendar. In this way, she could count the number of "1" days and the number of "5" days and see if the better days were increasing. The scale at the bottom includes the anchor points that help to ensure reliability of the data collection.

Sydney Bell Intensity Data Sheet **January 2016**

Sunday	Monday	Tuesday	Wednesday	Thursday	Friday	Saturday
					1	2
3	4 4	5 3	6 3	7 2	8 5	9
10	11 5	12 4	13 2	14 3	15 3	16
17	18 No school	19 5	20 2	21 2	22 5	23
24	25 2	26 3	27 4	28 2	29	30

1	2	3	4	5
No behavior incidents	Some whining, crying, pushing	Moderate – some hitting, crying, yelling	Biting, scratching for periods of time	Urinating, biting, scratching, inconsolable

Figure 5.8. Calendar rating system for intensity of challenging behavior.

Rating scales. Figure 5.9 shows the Intensity Rating Scale (Reeve & Carr, 2000), which was used to assess the prevention of escalation of intensity of behavior using functional communication training. The scale was validated by having teachers view videotapes of different intensities of behavior and rate the intensity of the behaviors by the anchors. The scale provides behavioral descriptors for each of the points on the scale. You would rate the behavior's intensity from 1-7 with anchors provided for 1 (Mild), 4 (Moderate,) and 7 (Serious). You could use this type of scale with a calendar like the example above, with a rating scale like those described below, or on its own for behaviors that do not occur frequently, using a page for each behavior.

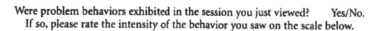

Were problem behaviors exhibited in the session you just viewed? Yes/No.
If so, please rate the intensity of the behavior you saw on the scale below.

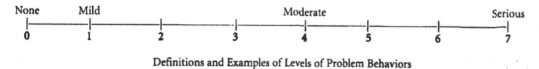

Definitions and Examples of Levels of Problem Behaviors

Problem behaviors involve (a) aggression, (b) whining/tantrums, (c) noncompliance, (d) property destruction, or (e) self-injury.

"0" No Problems

"1" Mild Problems

The intensity of these behaviors would not cause serious injury to the individuals or those around them. These behaviors would cause only minor disruption of ongoing activities.

Examples include (a) moving as if to slap someone, (b) whining, (c) getting out of seat, and (d) dropping or tossing object. (No self-injurious behavior is considered mild.)

"4" Moderate

The intensity of the behavior might cause some injury to the individual or others and/or some disruption of ongoing activities.

Examples include (a) slapping (wrist motion only), (b) crying, (c) standing on a table, (d) clearing table of objects by knocking them to floor, and (e) hitting head lightly against object or with hand.

"7" Serious

The intensity of the behavior is likely to cause serious injury to the individual or others and/or major disruption of ongoing activities.

Examples include (a) full-arm (over head) hitting, (b) repeated loud yelling or screaming, (c) (noncompliance is not considered serious unless other severe behaviors are occurring), (d) beating objects with hands or other objects hard enough to break them, and (e) self-directed hand-biting in which teeth marks are clearly visible.

Figure 5.9. Intensity rating scale.

Sometimes multiple variables, such as intensity and frequency, can be recorded on a rating scale. The one below is adapted from one published in Prevent Teach Reinforce (Dunlap et al., 2010). We have used it in a variety of ways including rating just intensity, rating intensity and frequency (as shown in Figure 5.11), and rating the overall impact of behavior on the day (e.g., (1) no challenging behavior, (3) moderate challenging behavior, (5) day disrupted with challenging behavior). The key is typically individualized to the student, but the one on this scale may be used in many situations. When the ratings are circled, they can be connected to create a graph of the student's behavioral progress (as shown in Figure 5.11). The data sheet typically contains two weeks of data on the top and two on the bottom, resulting in data collected for four weeks. In the example in Figure 5.10, The teacher circled the number of outbursts that occurred that day, providing a frequency count in the top row. This only works for a student who is unlikely to have more than five outbursts a day, which was true for Tyler. In the second row, the teacher rated the severity of the outburst using the key at the bottom of the scale.

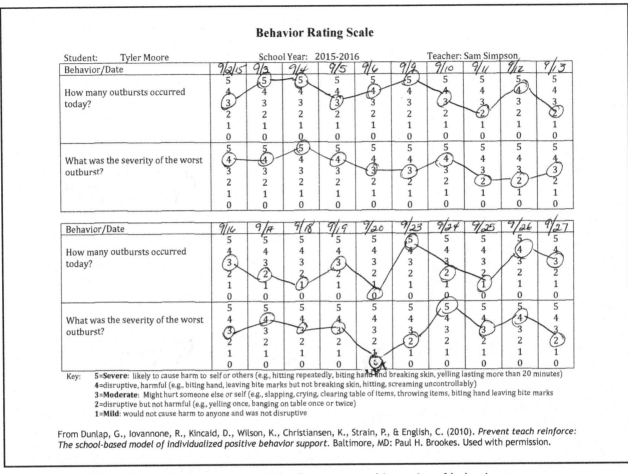

Figure 5.10. Self-graphing behavior rating chart for frequency and intensity of behavior.

Antecedent-Behavior-Consequence (ABC) Data

As mentioned, the reason for taking behavioral data influences the selection of the data collection tool. When the data is collected as part of an FBA, it is important to use an ABC data form. The purpose of completing an FBA is to examine behavior occurrences for patterns, and the ABC data sheet helps to accomplish that by providing information about the behavior in relation to what is happening in the environment around the individual. In ABC data, the A stands for antecedent, or what is happening before the behavior occurs; B refers to the actual behavior, defined in observable terms; and C is the consequence or what happens after the behavior, or how people respond to the individual after the behavior occurs.

For example, when given difficult math problems, the student rips his paper up and runs towards the classroom door. This response has occurred a number of times. If the teacher sends the student to the office, the student gets out of completing the difficult work. This would lead us to hypothesize that the student was exhibiting the behavior to escape task demands. If, on the other hand, all the other students stop what they are doing, look at the student, and yell out to the teacher to tell her the student is leaving the room, the hypothesis might be that the behavior served an attention-seeking function. Several examples of ABC data sheets are introduced here as options.

Fill-in ABC form. The ABC form in Figure 5.11 requires the person taking the data to describe, in narrative form, the behavioral incident in objective, behavioral terms – that is, the antecedent, the behavior itself, and the consequence of the behavior. Other information that is usually recorded includes the time the behavior occurred and the academic subject/activity that was taking place at the time of the behavior.

Fill-In ABC Assessment Form

Name: Naomi Johnson   **Date:** September 20, 2016   **Rater:** Sally McKenzie

Today the student is: ☑ Tired   ☐ Angry   ☐ Sad   ☐ Not feeling well   ☐ Easily agitated   ☐ Other _____

Describe any situations that you are aware of that might affect the student's behavior but may not be directly related in the data sheet below (e.g., he didn't like his choices for lunch today, but problems were not exhibited until recess; he didn't take his medication). _____

Mother reported that Naomi did not sleep well last night.

Date/ Time / Activity	What happened before the behavior?	What behavior occurred?	What happened after?
9/20/16 8:00 am Morning meeting	Ms. McKenzie was leading the calendar activity and all the children were given a turn to tell how they came to school.	When a classmate was called upon, Naomi jumped up, threw her chair over, and screamed. She then left the morning meeting area.	Ms. M. continued leading morning meeting and the aides left Naomi to calm down by herself. After a few minutes, one of the aides walked over to Naomi and directed her back to the morning meeting area, where she sat down.
9/20/16 10:30 am Reading center	The children in the small reading group were taking turns reading one page from the story. The teacher was correcting any errors. Naomi took her turn, and then it was time for another student to read.	Naomi ripped the book out of her classmate's hand while he was reading and threw it away from the reading area.	Naomi was ignored by the teacher who directed the child to continue reading from the teacher's copy of the story.

Figure 5.11. Fill-in ABC assessment form.

One advantage of this format is that it allows for rich descriptions. At the same time, however, there is the potential disadvantage that if the person completing the form is not skilled at writing in behavioral terms, the information presented may reflect his or her biases and predispositions.

Naomi was tired that day because she hadn't slept well the night before. This is a common setting event that may lead to problems later in the day when a trigger is encountered for behaviors. In the first instance, the teacher was teaching a group activity and called on a student. This directly preceded Naomi getting up and throwing her chair. This may or may not be a trigger, but the more information that is included in the antecedent and consequence data, the more likely it is that the team will be able to identify patterns. After Naomi threw the chair and left the group, the staff left her alone for a little while and then went over and redirected her back to the group.

In the second instance (starting at 10:30 am), a pattern might be beginning to emerge whereby the teacher attending to another student by not calling on Naomi or giving another student a turn may be a common antecedent for challenging behavior. Although the staff didn't think it was related and didn't report this pattern in interviews, the data may indicate that the teacher attending to someone else was a trigger for Naomi's challenging behavior.

It is important to remember that when using this type of data sheet, the more information that is recorded the fuller the picture will be for analysis. It is also important to ensure that the staff or families who complete the data sheet understand what they are to write. If they don't, the recorder may indicate that nothing happened after Naomi threw the chair rather than writing that she left the area, they left her alone, and then they approached her and brought her back to the group. Similarly, they may write that nothing happened because no one was interacting with Naomi before the behavior occurred when, in actuality, it might be that the fact that the adults were attending to others was the trigger that sparked the challenging behavior.

Check-off ABC form. For classroom staff who need a quicker (it takes time to write a narrative as in the fill-in ABC form), more efficient way to take ABC data, check-off formats are often preferable. As illustrated in Figure 5.13, the Antecedent column lists factors that often set the student up to demonstrate the behavior of concern. A range of behaviors that the student has exhibited in the past are listed under the Behavior column. Finally, common responses on the part of the staff and other students in the class are listed in the Consequence column. All you have to do is check off the appropriate items. Because the items have been selected to reflect the possible functions of behavior, it makes it easy to analyze the information to make hypotheses about the function(s) of behavior the student is exhibiting. In this case, Josephine was participating in a general education classroom, and her general education teacher usually collected the data. There was limited time for writing information out, so Sam used a version of the check-off ABC data sheet to record information and added notes when she could. Several versions of this form are available for downloading at https://www.aapcpublishing.net/bookstore/books/9123.aspx.

A-B-C Form (RTI Version)

Name: **Josephine Baker**	Observer: **Sam Simpson**		Target Behavior: See behavior column below	
Date	**Activity** (Fill in with activities specific to student)	**What was happening before or while the behavior occurred?** (Check all that apply)	**Behavior** (Check all that apply)	**What happened after the behavior?** (Check all that apply)	**Comments**

Date	Activity	What was happening before	Behavior	What happened after	Comments
9/1/2015	☐ Bathroom ☒ Recess ☐ Homeroom ☐ Hallway ☐ Lunchroom ☐ Reading ☐ Math ☐ Music ☐ Speech ☐ Science ☐ Social Studies ☐ _____	☐ Asked to work ☒ Given a direction ☐ Walking in hallway ☐ Waiting ☐ Working on task ☐ Assigned work with group ☐ Between activities ☒ Peer approached to interact ☐ Change in routine ☐ Corrected ☐ Entered classroom ☐ Other _____	☐ Insulted peer ☒ Didn't follow teacher's direction ☐ Verbally told teacher "no" ☒ Did not complete assigned task ☐ Got out the wrong materials ☐ Talking to peer (when not supposed to) ☐ Yelled in class ☒ Refuses to participate in group activity ☐ Participates in preferred activity ☐ Interferes with other students' activities ☐ Did not stop something when directed to ☐ Other _____	☒ Verbally redirected ☐ Verbally corrected ☐ Physically redirected ☐ Other student yelled/reprimanded her ☐ Other student interacted in some way ☐ Removed from setting ☐ Work demand adjusted ☒ Work demand withdrawn ☐ Redirected for a break ☐ Redirected to another activity/action ☒ New choices issued ☐ Other (Describe)	We asked her to join the game at recess, but she refused to participate. SS
9/2/2015	☐ Bathroom ☒ Recess ☐ Homeroom ☐ Hallway ☐ Lunchroom ☐ Reading ☐ Math ☐ Music ☐ Speech ☐ Science ☐ Social Studies ☐ _____	☒ Asked to work ☐ Given a direction ☐ Walking in hallway ☐ Waiting ☐ Working on task ☐ Assigned work with group ☐ Between activities ☐ Peer approached to interact ☒ Change in routine ☐ Corrected ☐ Entered classroom ☐ Other _____	☐ Insulted peer ☐ Didn't follow teacher's direction ☒ Verbally told teacher "no" ☐ Did not complete assigned task ☒ Got out the wrong materials ☐ Talking to peer (when not supposed to) ☒ Yelled in class ☐ Refuses to participate in group activity ☐ Participates in preferred activity ☐ Interferes with other students' activities ☐ Did not stop something when directed to ☐ Other _____	☒ Verbally redirected ☐ Verbally corrected ☐ Physically redirected ☐ Other student yelled/reprimanded her ☐ Other student interacted in some way ☒ Removed from setting ☐ Work demand adjusted ☒ Work demand withdrawn ☐ Redirected for a break ☐ Redirected to another activity/action ☐ New choices issued ☐ Other (Describe)	Josephine was asked to do her assignment in math. She was supposed to go to speech during that time, but the SLP was absent. She refused to participate, told me no and started yelling in class. SS
9/4/2015	☐ Bathroom ☒ Recess ☐ Homeroom ☐ Hallway ☐ Lunchroom ☐ Reading ☐ Math ☐ Music ☐ Speech ☐ Science ☐ Social Studies ☐ _____	☐ Asked to work ☐ Given a direction ☒ Walking in hallway ☒ Waiting ☐ Working on task ☐ Assigned work with group ☐ Between activities ☐ Peer approached to interact ☐ Change in routine ☐ Corrected ☐ Entered classroom ☐ Other _____	☐ Insulted peer ☐ Didn't follow teacher's direction ☐ Verbally told teacher "no" ☐ Did not complete assigned task ☐ Got out the wrong materials ☐ Talking to peer (when not supposed to) ☐ Yelled in class ☐ Refuses to participate in group activity ☐ Participates in preferred activity ☒ Interferes with other students' activities ☐ Did not stop something when directed to ☒ Other: _Hit the girl next to her with her hand_	☐ Verbally redirected ☒ Verbally corrected ☐ Physically redirected ☒ Other student yelled/reprimanded her ☐ Other student interacted in some way ☒ Removed from setting ☐ Work demand adjusted ☐ Work demand withdrawn ☐ Redirected for a break ☐ Redirected to another activity/action ☐ New choices issued ☐ Other (Describe)	Josephine hit Susie on the back of the head with an open palm while waiting in line for the bathroom. Susie started to cry and I reprimanded Josephine, removed her from the line and sent her back to class. SS

Figure 5.12. Check-off ABC data form (RTI version).

Scatterplot

A scatterplot is used to determine whether there is a pattern to the time/activity in which challenging behaviors occur. It is often used in FBAs to determine setting events or antecedents that are influencing the occurrence of these behaviors.

In a scatterplot, the behavioral occurrences are tracked over the scheduled periods of the day (e.g., morning meeting, guided reading small group, recess, story time, specials, lunch, small group leisure skill rotations, snack, and afternoon meeting) or the time of day. The behavioral data may also be graphed in accordance with certain conditions, (e.g., nights the student slept well and nights the student slept poorly, or Mondays versus other days of the week). The data sheet presented in Figure 5.13 allows you to record both the target behaviors you are trying to decrease (e.g., hitting) and replacement behaviors (e.g., asking for help) you are trying to increase. The shaded areas are times when Spence was not in the setting so no data could be taken. The Xs indicate times of day when the behavior occurred at least one time.

Scatterplot Data Collection

Directions: Put a tally mark or X in the interval if a target and/or replacement behavior occurred during that time period.

Name: **Spence Dawson**	Date: **9/3/15**	Teacher: Jenny Davis

Target Behavior: Challenging behavior comprised of hitting and kicking—Physical contact between Spence's hand or foot and the body of another student or teacher
Replacement Behavior: Requesting help or requesting a break

Target Behaviors						Replacement Behaviors					
Behavior **Time**	Hit	Kick			OTHER	**Behavior** **Time**	Ask for help	Ask for a break			OTHER
8:00-8:15						8:00-8:15					
8:15-8:30						8:15-8:30					
8:30-8:45						8:30-8:45	X				
8:45-9:00						8:45-9:00					
9:00-9:15						9:00-9:15					
9:15-9:30						9:15-9:30		X			
9:30-9:45	X	X				9:30-9:45					
9:45-10:00						9:45-10:00					
10:00-10:15						10:00-10:15					
10:15-10:30						10:15-10:30					
10:30-10:45						10:30-10:45	X	X			
10:45-11:00						10:45-11:00					
11:00-11:15						11:00-11:15					
11:15-11:30						11:15-11:30					
11:30-11:45						11:30-11:45					
11:45-12:00						11:45-12:00	X				
12:00-12:15		X				12:00-12:15					
12:15-12:30						12:15-12:30		X			
12:30-12:45						12:30-12:45					
12:45-1:00						12:45-1:00					
1:00-1:15						1:00-1:15	X				
1:15-1:30						1:15-1:30					
1:30-1:45						1:30-1:45					
1:45-2:00	X					1:45-2:00					
2:00-2:15						2:00-2:15					
2:15-2:30						2:15-2:30					
2:30-2:45						2:30-2:45					
2:45-3:00						2:45-3:00					
3:00-3:15						3:00-3:15					
Total	2	2				**Total**	4	3			
Percent	8	8				**Percent**	17	13			

Date	Comments/Observations
9/3/15	Left at 2:00 for a doctor's appointment

Figure 5.13. Scatterplot data sheet.

As illustrated, Spence exhibited hitting at least once during two intervals and kicking at least once during two intervals. It's important to recognize that this does not equate to the frequency being two. Instead it indicates that behavior occurred at least once during two intervals or for 8% of the intervals. The behavior may have occurred multiple times within an interval but it would only be recorded once. The data are typically reported as a percentage of intervals in which the behavior or skill occurred. In Spence's case, he asked for a break on 17% of the intervals on this day.

Chapter 6
Analyzing Challenging Behavior Data

Overview

It is important to analyze information collected about challenging behavior for two reasons: (a) to understand what function(s) the behavior is serving and (b) to determine whether the interventions that are put in place to address challenging behavior are effective.

- What graphing procedures allow you to analyze ABC data to determine the function(s) of a behavior?

- Can you use a self-graphing data sheet that allows you to visually inspect the person's progress towards reducing challenging behavior?

- What procedures or tools will help you summarize data that allows you to make decisions about the effectiveness of interventions?

- How does technology help to analyze data for your use?

Just as with skill acquisition data, it is important to analyze the data that you are collecting on a student's challenging behaviors. This chapter provides information about how to make decisions about why behaviors are occurring and identify the functions they are serving. This allows you to determine whether a behavior plan is being successful in addressing challenging behaviors.

Evaluating Data for a Functional Behavior Assessment

When performing an FBA, information is collected from a variety of people and in a variety of formats to get a complete picture of the student and any behavior problems. Some of that information comes from interviews with knowledgeable informants; other information is obtained by completing questionnaires (e.g., the Motivation Assessment Scale; Durand & Crimmins, 1988) or conducting reinforcer assessments. These types of information are not considered data in the sense that we are using the term in this book and, therefore, will not be discussed in further detail.

Data described earlier in the book that is useful for an FBA include ABC data, scatterplots, and other measures of behavior such as frequency, duration, and intensity. The data should provide solid information that tells you (a) who is most likely to be present when the behavior occurs, (b) what is going on when the behavior occurs, (c) when the behavior is most likely to occur, and (d) where the behavior is most likely to occur (Dunlap et al., 2010). In order to see the patterns in the behavior data that allow us to answer these questions, the behavior should be graphed. The type of graph used depends on the type of data that is being collected (e.g., frequency or rate data would be presented by a line graph while elements of ABC data would be presented by a bar graph).

The questions you are asking about a student's behavior lead you to the way you would graph the data obtained when taking ABC data. The questions include: (a) Are there common antecedents of the behavior? (b) Are there common consequences of the behavior? (c) Is it helpful to pinpoint which classes or settings have more frequent problem behaviors? (d) Is it helpful to consider common situations such as downtime or transitions that might play a factor? (e) Can you classify the functions of the individual behavior incidents? and (e) Are there setting events that should be evaluated and analyzed with regard to the challenging behavior?

Analyzing antecedent data. Review the data to determine if certain items can be grouped together and classified as having common elements, which would give you an idea of what most commonly precedes the behavior – the antecedent – and what triggers it. It is important to look for patterns rather than relying on just one incident. Creating a bar graph that summarizes the number of ABC instances that have common antecedents allows you to evaluate what antecedent types most commonly precede challenging behavior episodes. As a result of this analysis, you may get information about what antecedents need to be altered to reduce the challenging behavior. In the following example (see Figure 6.1) of ABC data graphed on a limited number of antecedents, transitioning was the most common antecedent to the behavior.

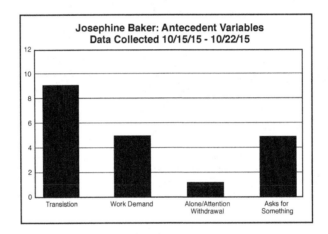

Figure 6.1. ABC data.

In some cases, a graph may be needed that breaks the antecedents down into more discrete categories or in which more antecedents are presented in the data, like the graph in Figure 6.2. In this case, demands were the most common antecedents, followed by waiting and sitting in groups.

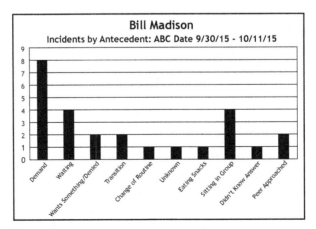

Figure 6.2. ABC data graphed by antecedent.

Analyzing consequence data. The consequence data from the ABC data sheet gives you information about what commonly happens in the environment after the behavior. Again, looking at patterns rather than the individual episodes is a key element, and a bar graph will allow you to see which types of social consequences are most associated with the behaviors being assessed. This may help to assess what may be reinforcing or maintaining the behavior over time (e.g., attention). Figures 6.3 and 6.4 provide examples of consequence data bar graphs. In Figure 6.3, being redirected or reprimanded was the most common consequence, which may indicate that attention from adults may be a maintaining reinforcer for this behavior. In Figure 6.4, being verbally and physically redirected were the two most common consequences with removal from the situation being third.

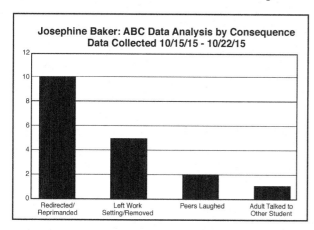

Figure 6.3. Josephine Baker's ABC data graphed by consequence.

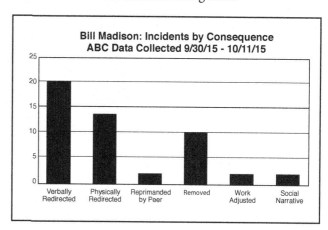

Figure 6.4. Bill Madison's ABC data graphed by consequences.

Analyzing data by setting. It may also be important to pinpoint which classes or settings are associated with frequent problems (see Figure 6.5). Graphing data by this variable may provide information about something that is specific to a given class or setting, including the instructor, peers, the group activities, and where the student is seated. It may also provide information about where it is most important to provide interventions. In Figure 6.5, it is clear that Bill exhibited the most challenging behavior during whole-group instruction. This fits with the antecedent data of downtime and waiting as well as consequence data (see Figure 6.4), and suggests that he is removed from whole-group activities when challenging behaviors occur.

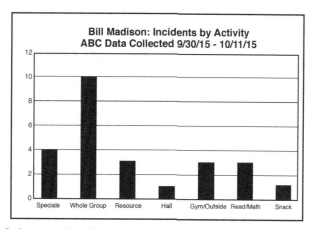

Figure 6.5. Bill Madison's ABC data graphed by activity.

Sometimes a student has more behavioral difficulty in one type of situation than in others. For instance, many students with ASD demonstrate more challenging behavior during waiting, downtime, or during transitions. It is important to analyze the ABC data to identify if many of the antecedent statements reflect that the learner was transitioning between activities when the behavior occurred or that there was not much going on in the environment when the behavior took place. Also, it is important to consider whether the behavior tended to occur when certain types of activities were going on (e.g., those that required a lot of writing). In that case, you might want to graph those elements, as in Figure 6.6. For Josephine, downtime was a significant factor for her challenging behavior, more so than transition, play or academics.

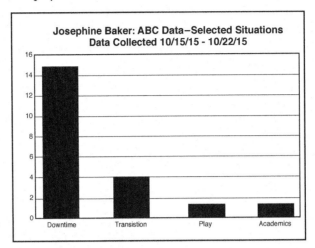

Figure 6.6. Josephine Baker's ABC data graphed by selected situations.

The purpose of an FBA is to develop hypotheses about the functions of behavior. Hypotheses are developed based on the data as the best guess of the possible triggers and the consequences that seem to be maintaining the behavior, such as escaping from a work demand or seeking the attention of an adult. It is helpful to graph the ABC data in terms of what you think may be the functions of the behavior incident that occurred. If the function is not clear to you, you may be better off reviewing some of the other graphs discussed and interpreting them to gain information and develop hypotheses about the function(s). For Bill, whose data is graphed in Figure 6.7, escape was clearly the most prevalent hypothesized function of his challenging behavior, which fit with the other data reviewed. The graphs of Bill's antecedent data (Figure 6.2) and data by activity (Figure 6.5) indicated that the most common situation in which Bill demonstrated challenging behavior was during activities with work demands and waiting in whole groups. His consequences graph (Figure 6.4) showed that he was most frequently physically and verbally redirected but that he was also removed from the situation at times. The educational team indicated that frequently the redirection was unsuccessful and that Bill had to be removed from the setting to calm down. Based on this information, the team determined that escaping from situations was a primary function of his challenging behavior.

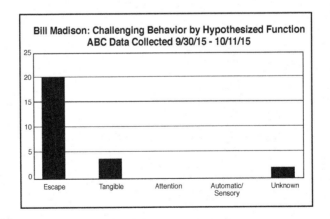

Figure 6.7. Bill Madison's ABC data graphed by hypothesized function.

Because escape was such a significant function, the team thought it would be helpful to determine in which specific situations Bill was most likely to engage in the challenging behaviors. To do so, they broke the data into more discrete categories of escape (e.g., escape from work demands, escape from whole group instruction) to see if there was a pattern (see Figure 6.8). It appeared that escaping from work was the function of the highest frequency of episodes. The team hypothesized that the expectations for Bill in groups were uncertain since the second highest frequency of episodes occurred to escape from groups. This helped the team to develop hypotheses of Bill's challenging behavior in order to develop a behavior plan that included replacement skills (i.e., asking for a break) that served the same function as the challenging behavior (i.e., escape).

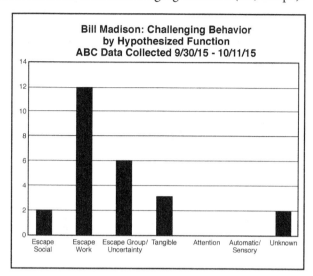

Figure 6.8. Bill Madison's ABC data graphed by more specific escape functions.

Setting events are events that increase the likelihood that a behavior will occur following an antecedent, although they may not occur close to the behavior in time. Examples include taking or missing medication, getting a poor night's sleep, feeling sick, having a fight with a parent before school, or being bullied by peers. It is helpful to look at the data in terms of potential setting events that the team has identified through interviews. For instance, graphing data by days that a parent reported a child did and did not sleep well might assess the impact of sleep on the behavior each day. Setting events can also be graphed from ABC data if there is information on the data sheet for setting events, such as the ABC data sheet included in Figure 5.11.

For Josephine, her team voiced concern that her behavior seemed very variable, with antecedents setting behavior off one day and resulting in no problem the next. The unpredictability was thought to possibly stem from the presence of setting events, so the data sheet was set up to assess some of the factors the team thought would be relevant. As illustrated in Figure 6.9, poor sleep and having a crisis earlier in the day were both noted as being involved in several incidents. However, in a number of incidents, no setting events were identified that day, suggesting that setting events most likely did not account for all the episodes of challenging behavior.

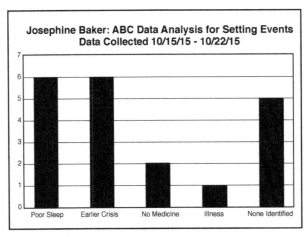

Figure 6.9. Josephine Baker's ABC data analyzed by setting events.

Scatterplot

Scatterplot data provide information about the settings and situations in which a behavior occurs. It can also be evaluated to determine if the behavior occurs more frequently during a specific time of day or in a specific place. The scatterplot in Figure 6.10 was created from ABC data of a kindergartner's behavior to assess if his tantrums occurred more frequently in the resource classroom or the kindergarten classroom and if it changed across the day. It was a powerful tool for the team to use to pinpoint the areas where intervention was most needed and to further assess the variables playing a role in the behavior. The shaded boxes indicate the presence of behavior with the number of instances written in the cell. This allowed the evaluator to see that the behavior occurred most frequently in the kindergarten classroom.

	Resource	Kindergarten	Art	Hall	Gym	Speech
2/1/2016		1				
3/2/2016		1				
3/9/2016	1					
4/4/2016	2					
4/5/2016	4	1				
4/6/2016	1					
4/12/2016	1	1				
4/13/2016	1	1	1			
4/21/2016		1				
4/26/2016		1				
4/27/2016		1				
4/29/2016		1				
5/2/2016		1				
5/3/2016						1
5/5/2016		1		1		
5/9/2016				1	1	
5/10/2016						1
5/11/2016				1		
5/12/2016		1				1

Figure 6.10. Scatterplot by setting for kindergarten student.

Monitoring the Success of a Behavior Intervention Plan (BIP)

Once a BIP has been developed based on a functional assessment, procedures must be put in place to monitor whether the plan is working. Usually, that is done by using one or a combination of the data collection strategies discussed in Chapter 5 (e.g., frequency, rate, duration, time sampling) depending upon which of these makes the most sense for the targeted behavior. For instance, hitting might be assessed using a partial interval data system whereas crying might be assessed using duration. The team should set a schedule for data review and for revising the BIP if it is not effective at reducing the target behaviors. In addition to data collected on the reduction of challenging behavior, data should be collected on skills that are targeted for acquisition as part of the behavior plan. If those skills are not increasing, the behavior may not decrease. Decisions regarding that data should follow the guidelines presented in Chapter 4. An easy way to track frequency data is to use the self-graphing rating data sheet shown in Figure 5.11 and repeated in Figure 6.11 below.

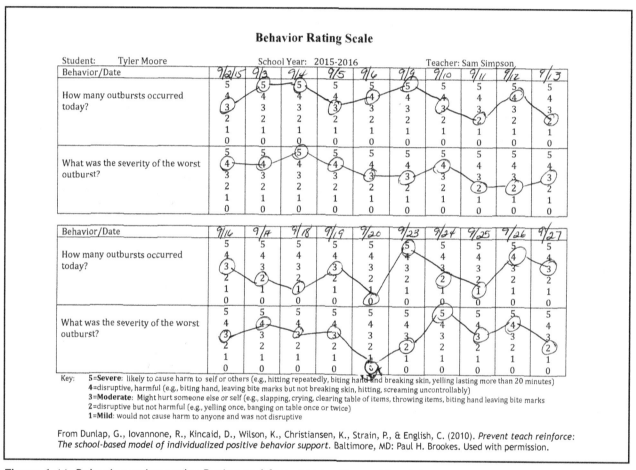

Figure 6.11. Behavior rating scale: Rating and frequency self-graphing data.

As illustrated, Tyler's frequency and severity of behavior is highly variable throughout the four weeks of data collection.

The graph in Figure 6.12, on the other hand, shows a trendline (the dashed diagonal line) indicating that the challenging behavior is decreasing from an average of 10 instances at the beginning of data collection to a mean under 5 instances by the end of data collection.

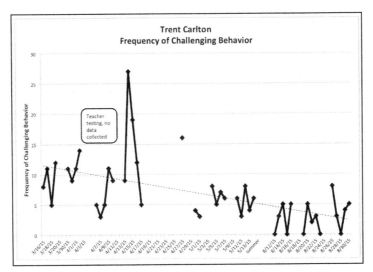

Figure 6.12. Frequency graph with decreasing trendline.

Overall, analysis of data for developing and monitoring behavior plans is a matter of organizing and presenting the data in a way that helps to draw conclusions and build hypotheses. As demonstrated throughout the chapter, this process may require graphing the data in a variety of ways to help to do that. Usually when team members can see the data depicted in a graphic form, it becomes easier to identify what variables play a role in the function of the challenging behavior and whether the behavior plan developed is working effectively.

Taking the time to analyze behavioral data is critical to evaluating the effectiveness of behavior reduction strategies, whether they include goals and objectives in an IEP or a BIP developed to reduce challenging behaviors. The importance of reviewing the effectiveness of a plan in reducing these behaviors as well as increasing replacement and other collateral skills (i.e., skills that do not replace the function of the behavior but also need to be taught, such as following teacher directions) cannot be overstated. It is critical that problem solving to identify additional strategies to implement take place in a timely manner to support an individual in need.

Chapter 7
Organizational Strategies for Data Collection and Analysis

Overview

Whether you work in a classroom, group home, or on a job site, in order to be successful in collecting and analyzing data, you must put organizational strategies in place.

- Have you selected appropriate data collection instruments and do you know how to use them?

- Have you trained other staff to take data reliably?

- Have you set time aside to analyze the data and change your instruction or behavior change strategies?

- Is data collection embedded into the ongoing operation of the environment?

- Do staff responsible for data collection know when and how to collect data (i.e., zoning plan)?

In our experience and work with education professionals, data collection, analysis, and use are the hardest tasks for staff to manage. While a lot has been written about the technical aspects of data collection and analysis, much less has been written about the practical aspects. Thus, there are few resources for helping teachers figure out how to implement adequate and useful data collection within their school day without losing their teaching time with the students. Instructors frequently comment that they have difficulty managing the paper or data collection tools at the same time they are trying to keep their students engaged. A major focus of this book is to help teachers figure out how to integrate the guidelines for good data collection and analysis with practical tools for getting it done.

What Data Do You Need?

One of the questions that many teachers ask is how to determine what data is needed and how to ensure that there is data on each skill being addressed in the program. Many general educators use curriculum checklists, such as those for the Common Core Curriculum (www.corestandards.org), to assess and ensure that students are mastering the curriculum goals. This type of checklist might be appropriate for students who are working on the general education standards. In some states, the extended, access, or alternate standards outline what each student in each grade using the alternate curriculum is required to master. For students who are working on alternate standards, several other curriculum tools might be helpful (e.g., http://www.cpalms.org/Public/search/Access-Point#0). A curriculum checklist for this type of assessment would be useful as well.

Further, the teacher might use a curriculum-based assessment such as the STAR curriculum (Arick et al., 2004), the ULS (https://www.n2y.com/products/unique), or the LINKS curriculum (http://www.linkscurriculum.com) – three curricula often found in classrooms for students with significant disabilities. These curriculum-based measures are coordinated with the Common Core Standards and most of the states' standards. They can be used to assess skills on the alternative curriculum on a monthly or quarterly basis to determine students' progress in the curriculum. These tools also serve to provide a guide and lessons for teaching the elements of the alternate curriculum.

In addition to the overall curriculum, each student who has an IEP also has annual goals and objectives. Data must be collected on each of these in order to report quarterly progress to parents or guardians. Each student's IEP must be operationalized so that the classroom staff know what data must be taken and how frequently in order to report progress. The CAPS (Henry & Myles, 2013), which was introduced in Chapter 1, is an instrument that does just that. Each IEP goal/objective is listed along with the activity/subject that is the primary area in which the skill will be taught, the teaching strategy that will be used to teach the skill, opportunities for the student to use the skill throughout the day to ensure generalization, and what data collection technique and frequency are needed to measure the criteria listed in the IEP. (There are other elements of the CAPS, but they don't relate to the data collection discussion.)

Comprehensive Autism Planning System (CAPS)

Child/Student: Sarah Chisolm   Date: 8/25/15

Time	Activity	Targeted Skills to Teach	Structure/ Modifications	Reinforce-ment	Sensory Strategies	Communication Social Skills	Data Collection	Generaliza-tion Plan
8:45-9:45	Math with Ms. Leslie	– Complete the math curriculum with modifications – Demonstrating number sense and place – Solve problems involving fractions and decimals – Add, subtract, multiply, divide with accommodations	– Reread directions – Break assignments into smaller increments – Checklists for doing her work – Extended time – Modified curriculum – Reduced content – Graphic organizers – Multiplication table grid reading materials aloud	Reinforcer inventory	– Opportunities to make sure her pencil is correct – Ability to fix the calendar or materials in the room – Opportunity to get erasers as needed	– Using communication to indicate when she needs assistance	– Work product – Checklist product	– Fade aide assistance as possible
9:45-10:45	English with Ms. Cale with support from Mr. Bryan	– Write more coherent sentences – Working independently in the context of a group and without direct adult supervision – Capitalize beginnings of sentences and use ending punctuation – Compose with proper punctuation – Use appropriate grammar in composition	– Graphic organizers – Independent work system for work completion – Modified grammar assignments – Rule sheets available – Reduced number of items – Reread instructions	– Reinforcer assessment	– Opportunities to make sure her pencil is correct – Ability to fix the calendar or materials in the room – Opportunity to get erasers as needed	– Using communication to indicate when she needs assistance – Visual supports/ reminders for attention requests,	– Work product, checklist	

Modified from Henry, S.A., & Myles, B.S. (2013). *The Comprehensive Autism Planning System (CAPS) for individuals with autism spectrum and related disabilities: Integrating evidence-based practices throughout the student's day* (2nd ed.). Shawnee Mission, KS: AAPC Publishing.

Figure 7.1. Sarah Chisholm's CAPS.

Figure 7.1 shows the elements and how the data collection assists the teacher in developing the right data tracking sheets to use to measure the skills in each student's CAPS. Sarah's day is outlined by the activities on her schedule. Sam uses the CAPS to determine which skills (IEP goals/objectives and curriculum skills) will be addressed in each activity. This allows him to identify the structure and/or modifications she can have in each activity, what reinforcers will be used, and what types of support she needs. Finally, it gives the team information about what type of data collection is needed. For instance, from 8:45-9:45 Sara is in math class. In addition to the general education assessments of her progress in the class curriculum, Sarah's targeted skills will be assessed through work product and checklists. Therefore, her skills solving problems with fractions and decimals will be assessed by work she completes in class and the aide working with her knows to complete a work product label and place it on the back of her work periodically to collect data.

How Much Data Do You Need?

The amount of data needed depends upon the student for whom you are planning to collect data. At a minimum, you need to meet the data collection requirements defined in the IEP. For example, if a student has a goal that says he will follow one-step directions four out of five times over three consecutive days, the data collection system must allow for five data points per day, and the staff must be sure that they are taking data on that particular skill or step of a skill three days in a row. If a goal has a mastery criterion of 100% on a weekly probe for four consecutive weeks, then the staff only has to take one data point per week, but must track the skill for four consecutive weeks.

It is not uncommon for instructors to be responsible for 8-10 students who each has several IEP goals/objectives that need to be tracked. Therefore, it is critical that you have a way to plan the data collection in the classroom over time to ensure that the specific criteria for mastery are being met. Once a CAPS has been developed for each student, or you use some other system to define the data collection needs of each student's instructional program, you can assign the skills that must be tracked to each activity that occurs throughout the student's instructional day, as illustrated in Figure 7.2.

Where and When Should Data Be Taken?

The CAPS defines the primary teaching activity or period of the day when data must be collected for each of a student's IEP goals/objectives. It is important to remember that as a student masters a goal and the focus shifts to generalization of that skill across activities and materials, the data collection shifts to other activities where the skill that has been learned may be used. The instructor must integrate the information about the data each student's program requires with the classroom schedule and zoning plan to make sure that the teacher and the aides are prepared to collect the data for each student across the day. Some goals/objectives easily lead to decisions about where they should be assessed because they naturally fit into certain activities. For example, reading goals in the area of decoding would best be taught in small-group reading instruction with data collection taking place during that time. Goals in the area of social interaction might be best taught in small groups led by the speech-language pathologist with generalization occurring during lunch or recess. This process can be completed using the zoning plan seen in Figure 7.2.

Sally's Zoning Plan (Excerpt)

Time/Activity	Sally	Chrissy	Robert	Comments
7:30-8:15 Arrival/Breakfast	Start at cafeteria; bring back N and S, bathroom students as you are able	Start at cafeteria, remain in cafeteria until all students have arrived; then escort students to room	Start at cafeteria, remain in cafeteria until all students or most of students have arrived, then escort to class	
8:15-8:30 Table Tasks	Transition first students back to schedule and table tasks; man table tasks; take data on two students' targeted goals each day	Transition students back to classroom, check their schedule, and check into table tasks; begin to pull students for bathroom one to two at a time; toileting data for B and S	Transition students back to classroom, check their schedule, and check into table tasks; begin to pull students for bathroom one to two at a time; toileting data for B and S	
8:30-8:45 Journals	Supervise journals, help students complete their page and tell about it if they can	Continue to pull students to bathroom and assist with journals when available	Continue to pull students to bathroom and assist with journals when available	Work product data collection
8:45-9:00 Circle	Run circle	Prompt and assist all students, particularly S; take data on one designated student's targeted goals/day	Prompt and assist all students, particularly N; take data on one designated student's targeted goals/day	
9:00-9:15 Centers 1	Reading with C and S; take daily data	Individual work with B and A; take data on one student per day	Art with N and N; take data on one student per day	
9:15-9:30 Centers 2	Reading with N and N; take daily data	IW with C and S; take data on one student per day	Art with B and A; take data on one student per day	
9:30-9:45 Centers 3	Reading with B and A; take daily data	IW with N and N; set up table tasks; take data on one student per day	Art with C and S; take data on one student per day	Mon and Thurs C goes to speech
9:45-10:00 TT/BR	Pull students 1-2 at a time for bathroom; toileting data for B and S	Pull students 1-2 at a time for bathroom; toileting data for B and S	Supervise table tasks	
10:00-10:30 PE/Gym	Stay to make sure choice time is ready, then join PE	Accompany students to PE; take data on one student per day	Accompany students to PE; take data on one student per day	

Figure 7.2. Zoning plan for Sally's classroom.

The "when" question is best answered by analyzing the mastery criteria; that is, how many days per week data must be collected on a particular skill for an individual child, as described above in the answer to the "how much" question. If the data are needed to assess the effectiveness of a behavior plan and the teacher knows that the challenging behavior occurs most frequently in the afternoon, it does her no good to schedule data collection on that behavior during the morning time, even if she has additional staff available and, therefore, it would be most convenient. The teacher must find a way to record the incidents of the behavior in the afternoon.

Who Will Take the Data?

All staff in the classroom, as well as any other service providers in the school environment, must be trained to take the type of data that is necessary to answer the questions related to whether the student has met her IEP goals/objectives or behavioral targets. Everyone must feel comfortable with the data collection techniques being used so the task can be shared. In special education programs, for example, classroom or individually assigned aides often lead instruction and, therefore, become responsible for data collection during that time.

The zoning plan shown in Figure 7.2 was introduced in Chapter 1 for use in Sally's classroom. Zoning plans should always be developed by the classroom team so that staff members' preferences can be considered in terms of which activities each feels most comfortable leading. Once each staff person has been assigned to activities/subjects, students, and areas of the room, duties like area set-up and clean-up, student prompting and behavior support, and data collection can be assigned.

The zoning plan directly leads to a professional development plan for each staff member to ensure that he or she has the skills needed to meet his or her responsibilities delineated in the plan. The zoning plan may assign one of the paraprofessionals to take data during morning meeting, but then it is up to the teacher to determine how many days per week data on goals/objectives being targeted in morning meeting need to be collected for each student. Generally, it is useful to collect data several days per week for each goal/objective for each student. The ability to implement this will be impacted by the number of goals/objectives that fit into a particular activity and how many students are participating in the activity at the same time.

How Will Materials Be Organized?

It is important to find data collection procedures that work for you and your team. This requires advance planning and a great deal of organization. At the beginning of the school year, you must consider the data collection needs of each student and the classroom as a whole. It is easier to plan for 1:1, 1:2, or even 1:3 instruction, where an instructor can take data on 1-2 students each day and get 3 days of data for each learner. In that case, a basket of clipboards (see page 104) with each student's DTT programs stored will keep the data sheets organized. Some instructors have a basket of materials with a clipboard of data sheets for each student. That is useful when the goals/objectives that each learner is working on are very different.

It becomes more difficult when one person is taking data during a whole-class activity and must record data for 6-10 children. It is usually more effective when certain children or certain types of skills are targeted each day, and the instruction is planned so as to lead to multiple opportunities for responses of the target skill. Nevertheless, the more different the students' IEP goals/objectives are, the harder it is to differentiate instruction and collect data. In these situations, you will need to make a decision about whether to collect data samples, have another staff member collect the data, or use another tool (e.g., a counter).

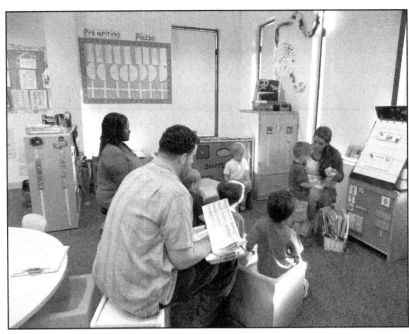

Figure 7.3. In this picture, Mike, the paraprofessional, is collecting data on a student's performance during morning meeting, which allows the teacher to conduct the activity.

Some teachers prefer to use data sheets for naturalistic data designed to measure skills in each area of the classroom for multiple children, as seen in Figure 7.4. That makes it easier because the skills of multiple students are listed on one data sheet so you don't have to flip through multiple data sheets.

Figure 7.4. A naturalistic sample data sheet-group.

Other instructors prefer for each student to have his or her own data sheet so that the data do not have to be transferred to another sheet or entered into a spreadsheet to be graphed for each learner as seen in Figure 7.5. If you choose this approach, the data sheet must move with the learner throughout the day, and the data collector may have to flip through several sheets to record data.

Naturalistic Sample Data Sheet

Student: Angie Harding **Teacher:** Sally McKenzie **Week:** 9/26/15

Direct Instruction	Circle	Play	Art / Games	Kindergarten
Request help verbally when needed	Raise her hand, wait to be called on with wait sign before making request	Request items/actions using a 2-3 word sentence	Follow directions from a peer in structured game	Raise her hand, wait to be called on with wait sign before making request
+ p + +	+ + p p	+ + p p	+ + +	p p + + p
Request items missing or needed	Follow instructions given to a group	Initiate play with a peer using language	Request items/actions using a 2-3 word sentence	Request help verbally when needed
p p + + p	+ p + p +	+ +	p + + +	+ +
Demonstrate consistent tripod grip when writing	Request desired items from peers	Look at her partner, wait for him to make eye contact, then make request	Request help verbally when needed	Follow instructions given to a group ++
+ +	p p + +	p p p +	+ p + p p	p p + p p
Maintain conversation for 3 turns	Maintain conversation for 3 turns	Request desired items from peers	Give and receive materials from peers independently	Maintain conversation for 3 turns
+ p	p + p	+ p + + +	+ p + p +	+ +
Walk in a line with peer without touching others (check off daily)	Request items/actions using a 2-3 word sentence	Ask for a turn when she wants to participate	Take turns with peer in a structure situation, give and receive materials	Walk in a line with peer without touching others (check off daily)
p + X p +	+ p + p +	+ + p + p	+ + + + +	+ p + + +

+ = Independent P = Promoted X = Incorrect 0 = No Response: a blank means there was no opportunity to exhibit the skill

Figure 7.5. Example of a naturalistic sample data sheet — individual.

Organizing the amount of paper for a data collection system can be a challenge within any learning environment. The following are examples of creative ways to organize the data collection within learning environments so that the required materials are close at hand and ready to access during instruction.

This teacher held a 1-1 or small-group instruction session at the table in the center of the classroom, which limited her ability to keep track of the data sheets since the table was used for multiple activities. To address this, she kept the data sheets (along with numerous pens!) in a basket on a shelf in the room and had a student bring them to the instructional area at the beginning of the center rotation. Each student had his or her own clipboard that contained the discrete trial programs he or she was working on.

This teacher organized materials for his small-group or 1-1 instructional center by storing both the data sheets and the materials needed for the programs in the same basket. Each student had his or her own basket for work time (e.g., Lance's and Sam's baskets), and other baskets held group curriculum tools (e.g., Phonics Readers, Time & Money Sheets) that all the students used.

Schedule visuals provided by The Picture Communication Symbols ©1981-2011 by Mayer-Johnson LLC. All Rights Reserved Worldwide. Used with permission. Boardmaker® is a trademark of Mayer-Johnson LLC.

This teacher posted a data sheet for specific lesson plans in groups on the back of the shelf in that particular area. Multiple students' names with their individualized goals were written on the sheet for data collection on a weekly basis.

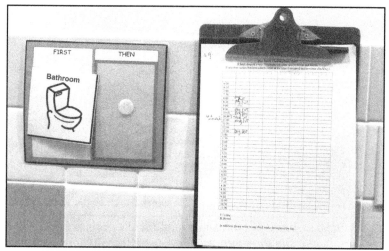

Bathroom visual created with The Picture Communication Symbols ©1981-2011 by Mayer-Johnson LLC. All Rights Reserved Worldwide. Used with permission. Boardmaker® is a trademark of Mayer-Johnson LLC.

This teacher posted the toileting data sheet on the wall in the bathroom to remind staff to take data on the student's toileting skills and behavior. It provided easy access to the sheet when the students were in the bathroom.

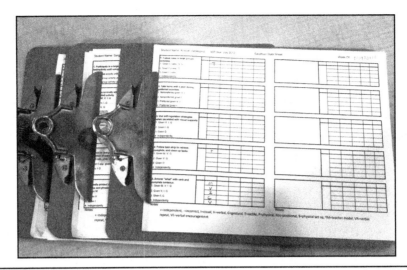

This picture shows data sheets for multiple students organized by group. Each clipboard holds a data sheet for each group at this activity, and the clipboards are set on the shelf overlooking the relevant area.

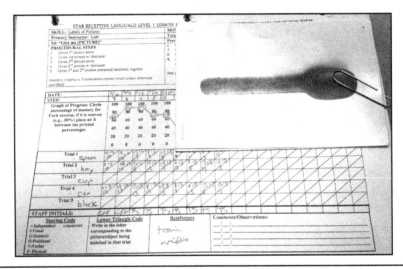

This teacher used a paperclip to attach pictures needed for discrete trials to the relevant data sheet programs so that the materials and data sheet were ready whenever she sat down to teach the student that skill from the data notebook.

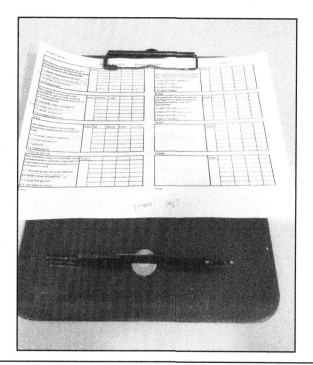

The teacher used Velcro® to attach the pen to the clipboard to make sure it was always available for data collection.

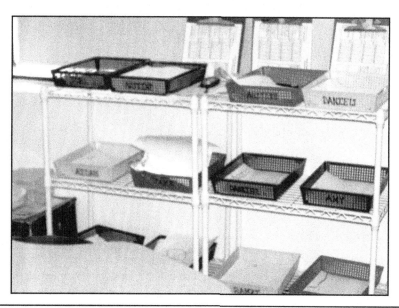

The teacher organized her data collection and materials by group. For each student, the basket of materials is organized in rows related to the groups. Clipboards with the data sheets for each group sit on the top shelf.

Visuals created by The Picture Communication Symbols ©1981-2011 by Mayer-Johnson LLC. All Rights Reserved Worldwide. Used with permission. Boardmaker® is a trademark of Mayer-Johnson LLC.

The teacher has all the materials and the data collection notebook in bins labeled with the students' names. Students are responsible for bringing the bin to the worktable when their schedule tells them to come to work with the teacher.

This picture shows a discrete trial area in an early intervention program. Each student is assigned a clipboard. The clipboards contain students' discrete trial data sheets along with any materials that can be clipped to the boards. Additional materials are pulled from the shelves and drawers as needed. The data sheets are laid out from left to right in the order in which the children rotate through the center.

The examples above work well for organizing and storing materials for data collection. A host of other options make data collection and documentation more portable within the classroom and the school as students and staff move around the activities of their day, as illustrated in the following.

These picture cards were used during discrete trial instruction. The learner's performance was tracked by putting the cards that the student answered correctly on the left and the cards that were incorrect or needed prompting on the right. When the student is working independently or has moved on to another activity, the teacher would quickly count the pictures in each pile and record the data.

The teacher recorded the data for each card on the back of the card. She had to combine all the cards to review the student's progress on the whole alphabet, but it was a quick and easy way to see which targets were being mastered. If the cards are laminated, a dry-erase pen may be used and the system reset for another student.

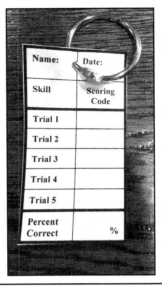

Keychain being used with the mix-and-vary discrete trial data sheets that were discussed in Chapter 3. The staff member records data for each opportunity for the student to practice the skill.

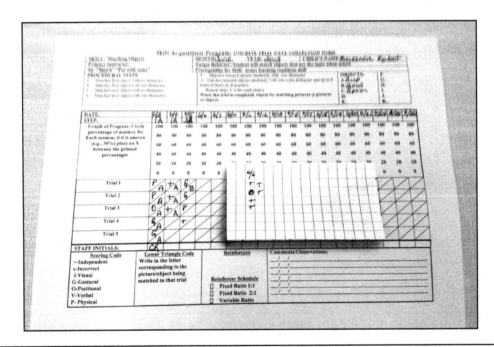

This instructor took data on a sticky note. She attached it to the data sheet corresponding to the targeted skill and transferred the data onto the form at the end of the day. She carried sticky notes in her pocket to use when she embedded her teaching into a naturalistic situation.

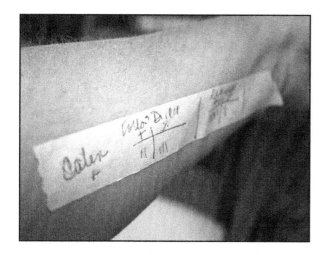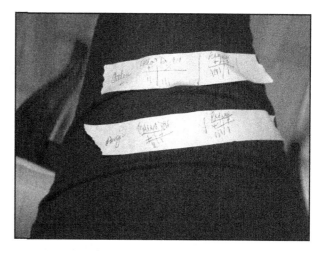

In these pictures the teacher used masking tape on her arm or leg to track the data. This allowed her to move around the room and sit in a group activity without a table and still record the data without having to keep track of a clipboard. She simply wrote the child's name and the skill she was tracking and divided rows for tally marks of correct and prompted or incorrect responses. The data was then transferred to a data sheet at the end of the day.

Counters are frequently used to track frequency. Each time the skill is performed, the recorder simply clicks the counter. At the end of the data collection period, the total shown on the clicker is recorded on a graph or data sheet. Counters may be purchased at office or teacher supply stores. Some teachers use multiple counters to track multiple skills simultaneously – different-colored counters keep skills straight while recording the data.

In recent years a number of developers have built apps for smartphones and tablets that increase the portability of wide ranges of types of data collection. The frequency with which these apps are developed and changed makes a thorough review beyond the scope of this book. However, a few examples are listed below.

Super Duper® Publications (http://www.superduperinc.com/products/view.aspx?stid=631#.VPydxIHF_UQ) has developed an app called Data Tracker that allows you to input students' names or initials, group them, and record a variety of information in real time, including tally or frequency, correct or incorrect responses (see below), and approximation and cue information.

Used with permission from Super Duper® Publications.

Use of the Data Tracker shows that Calen followed four of six directions given in morning meeting.

Behavior Tracker Pro (below) is another commonly used app that allows tracking frequency data, interval data and ABC data, and allows you to videotape observations as well.

Used with permission from Behavior Tracker Pro
(www.behaviortrackerpro.com).

Chapter 8
Case Study Solutions

Overview

In Chapter 1, we introduced three teachers and their teaching environments.
In this chapter, we revisit the three classrooms and see what data collection strategies they selected and how they applied them to their everyday practice.

It is now time to revisit the three teachers who were introduced at the beginning of this book: Sally, Sam, and Jenny. Each of these teachers faced different issues and challenges when planning data collection practices that would meet their needs.

Sally

Sally's students spend most of the day in her classroom, so she and her staff have the primary responsibility for collecting data on all academic and other skill areas being addressed, as well as behavior problems that are more likely to be exhibited by students placed in a self-contained classroom. Unlike Sam, who teaches general education and is responsible for a few students with ASD for part of the day, it is critical that Sally develop a CAPS for each of her students, as this will ensure that every goal/objective for each student is being addressed and data collection procedures for each are outlined. Sally's zoning plan is another element of classroom organization that ensures that all the classroom staff in a self-contained classroom know their data collection responsibilities. The zoning plan also lets Sally know what type of data collection procedures she needs to train her staff on in order to ensure that they are able to meet their assigned responsibilities in this area.

Once these foundations of classroom organization are in place, Sally must implement data collection systems that match the types of skill acquisition and behavior reduction targets she has defined for her students in their CAPS (Figure 2.4). Sally decided that she would use four types of data collection sheets for skill acquisition: the self-graphing Discrete Trial Program Data Sheet (Figure 3.4), the Naturalistic Sample Data Sheet for a group (Figure 3.7), the Task Analysis Data Sheet With Method (Figure 3.9), and the Toileting Data Sheet (Figure 3.10). She knows that keeping the naturalistic sample group data sheet in each of her instructional centers will require her to collect the data for each student and graph it using Excel, but she thinks it will be easier for her aides to keep track of just one data sheet in an area, instead of having to flip through other students' data sheets to record data.

Sally also has decided to use the Fill-In ABC Data Sheet With Setting Events (Figure 5.12) when taking data as part of a FBA because she thinks that will provide more information for her students with more complex behaviors. Once the function(s) of the behavior are discovered, she will have her staff take frequency data using the self-graphing Frequency Data Sheet (Figure 5.3), which will allow her to see whether the incidents of target behaviors are decreasing.

Sally is lucky because her paraprofessionals are paid for 30 minutes after the students leave. During that time, the paraprofessionals clean up, reset the classroom, and organize materials for the next day. On Thursdays, the staff use the time to enter the data collected over the course of the week on the group data sheets into the Excel template and graph the students' performance on each target. That gives them an opportunity to see the importance of data collection and includes them in the conversation about students who are making good progress, those who have reached a plateau, and those who are very inconsistent in their performance.

Sam

Sam, a general education teacher, has four students with IEPs in his classroom for part of the day. This means that he has to provide information about their performance on academic tasks, as well as social and behavioral goals/objectives. The special education case manager for his students has developed CAPS for the students (see Figure 7.1 for an example). Sam has a clear understanding of what skills he is targeting as well as what behaviors he needs to monitor. He feels confident about using worksheets but thinks that a percent correct score does not tell the entire story because he has to stand close to one of the students in order for him to perform and has to provide gestural prompts to get another student to continue to attend to the task. Myra, the autism consultant, has suggested that he use the computer-generated labels, which he places on the back of a sample of the students' worksheets to provide the information needed to judge whether each student is becoming more independent in his performance (see Figure 3.1 for a completed example).

Because Sam's students have sufficient cognitive abilities to be able to take responsibility for monitoring some of their own progress and behavior, they are taking travel cards between their classes and check off whether they turned in their homework, had their materials ready, took notes, and participated in class. Sarah Chisholm has an academic travel card (see Figure 8.1) that she takes to each of her classes and has the teacher complete at the end of the period. She then turns it into Sam at the end of each day.

Academic Travel Card

Name: Sarah Chisholm   **Week:** 9/14/15

	1st period	2nd period	3rd period	4th period	6th period	7th period
Monday	☐ Turn in homework ☑ Materials ready ☑ Took notes ☑ Participated	☑ Turn in homework ☑ Materials ready ☐ Took notes ☑ Participated	☑ Turn in homework ☑ Materials ready ☑ Took notes ☐ Participated	☑ Turn in homework ☐ Materials ready ☑ Took notes ☐ Participated	☑ Turn in homework ☑ Materials ready ☑ Took notes ☑ Participated	☑ Turn in homework ☑ Materials ready ☐ Took notes ☑ Participated
Tuesday	☑ Turn in homework ☑ Materials ready ☐ Took notes ☒ Participated	☑ Turn in homework ☐ Materials ready ☑ Took notes ☐ Participated	☑ Turn in homework ☐ Materials ready ☑ Took notes ☑ Participated	☑ Turn in homework ☐ Materials ready ☑ Took notes ☐ Participated	☑ Turn in homework ☑ Materials ready ☐ Took notes ☑ Participated	☐ Turn in homework ☑ Materials ready ☑ Took notes ☐ Participated
Wednesday	☒ Turn in homework ☑ Materials ready ☑ Took notes ☐ Participated	☑ Turn in homework ☑ Materials ready ☑ Took notes ☐ Participated	☑ Turn in homework ☑ Materials ready ☑ Took notes ☐ Participated	☑ Turn in homework ☑ Materials ready ☐ Took notes ☑ Participated	☑ Turn in homework ☑ Materials ready ☑ Took notes ☑ Participated	☑ Turn in homework ☐ Materials ready ☑ Took notes ☐ Participated
Thursday	☑ Turn in homework ☑ Materials ready ☑ Took notes ☑ Participated	☑ Turn in homework ☑ Materials ready ☐ Took notes ☑ Participated	☑ Turn in homework ☑ Materials ready ☑ Took notes ☑ Participated	☑ Turn in homework ☑ Materials ready ☑ Took notes ☐ Participated	☐ Turn in homework ☐ Materials ready ☒ Participated	☐ Turn in homework ☒ Took notes ☑ Participated
Friday	☑ Turn in homework ☑ Materials ready ☑ Took notes ☑ Participated	☑ Turn in homework ☑ Materials ready ☑ Took notes ☑ Participated	☑ Turn in homework ☑ Materials ready ☑ Took notes ☐ Participated	☑ Turn in homework ☑ Materials ready ☐ Took notes ☑ Participated	☑ Turn in homework ☑ Materials ready ☑ Took notes ☑ Participated	☑ Turn in homework ☑ Materials ready ☑ Took notes ☑ Participated
Totals	13/20	13/19 NO HW MON	12/19 NO HW MON	11/20	16/16	11/16
Comments	1st period - Tues - participation was yelling out + arguing Thurs - checked out early					

Figure 8.1. Travel card.

Sam was concerned that taking data on social and behavioral skills would be too time consuming. But Myra showed him how to use checklists and rubrics to keep track of the development of skills in those areas, which would not take too much time, yet would provide the information needed to evaluate whether a student was making adequate progress. To assess Susi's communication skills with her peers, Sam completed a weekly rubric (found in Figure 3.11) assessing her pragmatic skills. For Sarah, he developed an individualized weekly checklist (see Figure 8.2) based on her IEP goals for independence and social skills.

Weekly Data Checklist

Name: *Sarah Chisholm*	Date: *9/16/15*
Data Collector: *Mary Randall*	Teacher: *Sam Simpson*

Initiation and Responding to Peer

Check all that apply—I=Independent P=Prompted	I / P (Circle)	No Response	Inappropriate Response	Comments
1. Initiate interaction with peer (e.g., says hi)	I /**(P)**			
2. Respond to 1st peer statement	**(I)**/ P			
3. Respond to 2nd peer statement	**(I)**/ P			
4. Respond to 3rd peer statement	I /**(P)**			

Check all that apply—I=Independent P=Prompted	I / P (circle)	No Response	Inappropriate Response	Comments
1. Initiate interaction with peer (e.g., says hi)	**(I)** P			
2. Respond to 1st peer statement	**(I)**/ P			
3. Respond to 2nd peer statement	I /**(P)**		✓	"I don't want to."
4. Respond to 3rd peer statement	I / P	✓		

Independence Goal

Walking in Hallway	Number of redirections	Comments
1. Social Studies or Science: Walked in the hallway without aide, count number of redirections	1	great day!
2. Speech: Walked in hallway without aide, count number of redirections	0	

Locating Materials	Did it independently	# of redirections needed	Comments
1. Locate correct materials on list		2	
2. Turned to correct section in binder	✓		

Figure 8.2. Weekly data checklist.

In terms of behavior data, Sam generally felt that the check-off ABC data sheet would be easy to use and give him information about the conditions under which the behavior was likely to occur (see Figure 5.13). However, he was worried about the intensity of the behavior of one of his students. So once the functions of his students' behaviors were determined through an FBA, Myra suggested a scale that would measure intensity, the Behavioral Rating Scale in Figure 8.3.

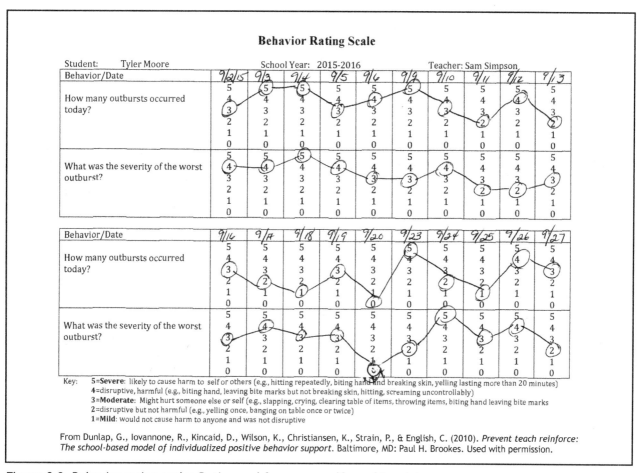

Behavior Rating Scale

Student: Tyler Moore School Year: 2015-2016 Teacher: Sam Simpson

Key: **5=Severe**: likely to cause harm to self or others (e.g., hitting repeatedly, biting hand and breaking skin, yelling lasting more than 20 minutes)
  4=disruptive, harmful (e.g., biting hand, leaving bite marks but not breaking skin, hitting, screaming uncontrollably)
  3=Moderate: Might hurt someone else or self (e.g., slapping, crying, clearing table of items, throwing items, biting hand leaving bite marks
  2=disruptive but not harmful (e.g., yelling once, banging on table once or twice)
  1=Mild: would not cause harm to anyone and was not disruptive

From Dunlap, G., Iovannone, R., Kincaid, D., Wilson, K., Christiansen, K., Strain, P., & English, C. (2010). *Prevent teach reinforce: The school-based model of individualized positive behavior support.* Baltimore, MD: Paul H. Brookes. Used with permission.

Figure 8.3. Behavior rating scale: Rating and frequency self-graphing data.

Jenny

Jenny was spending much of her time in the community on job sites and sites where her students could learn independent-living skills. That meant her data collection system had to be portable and easy to use in a variety of settings. She was intrigued by the idea of using a zoning plan to assign job coaches and paraprofessionals in the community to students. The assignments for each student were different depending upon the day of the week, as some students were on job sites one day a week, others for three days a week, and still others, for five days a week. She needed a different zoning plan for each day of the week (see an example in Figure 2.3).

She also needed to make sure that there were data collection systems in place in the classroom, as students spent between 25-50% of their time in the classroom. One of the strategies consisted of posting a scoring code for data collection on the wall near the work station so that the aides could just glance up and know how to code their data (see Figure 1.14).

It was important for Jenny to train her paraprofessionals to use data sheets that were designed for functional routines or for skills taught using task analysis. Many of the types of job assignments her students had in the community involved multiple steps so the Task Analysis Data Sheet With Method met her data collection needs (see Figure 3.9). The steps to the task were listed along with the directions for getting the student to complete the step so that a job coach or paraprofessional would be able to know exactly how to support the student to complete the task.

Some of the students in Jenny's class had the skills necessary to be taught to self-monitor. Myra suggested that she teach the students, who were not out in the community, to use the Incredible 5-Point Scale (Buron & Curtis, 2012) to monitor their participation throughout the day in each of their classes (see Figure 8.4). For students who were out on job sites, she suggested a 3-point rating scale for rating their performance during daily job training. This rating scale included the soft skills that individuals with ASD often have trouble with on job sites.

Incredible 5-Point Scale
Self-Monitoring

Name:	Date:

This is how I am feeling at the start of the period.

1 = I am really glad to be here. I will participate and I may even be able to help others.
2 = I am glad to be here and I will participate.
3 = I am here but I might not participate.
4 = I am here but I will not participate. I will not disrupt.
5 = I will not participate and I may disrupt if I have to stay in the room.

	Monday	Tuesday	Wednesday	Thursday	Friday
Period 1					
Period 2					
Period 3					
Period 4					
Period 5					
Period 6					
Period 7					
Comments					

Figure 8.4. Self-regulation data sheet.

Jenny also needed a way to assess students' job performance while they were out in the community or around the school. Some of her students were learning to monitor their own behavior and she wanted to teach them to reflect upon their work. The daily job training data sheet (Figure 8.5) allowed the worker, supervisor, and job coach to rate the worker's performance so that Jenny could determine if the worker was ready to self-monitor.

Daily Job Training
How Did I Do Today?

Name: Spence Dawson	Date: 10/16/15
Job Site: ABC Grocery Store	On-site Supervisor: Cathy Reed
School Job Coach: Vicki Smith	

Rating Scale:
3 Excellent (e.g., independent, high quality)
2 Adequate (e.g., some prompts, acceptable quality)
1 Poor (e.g., did not complete, needed significant help, poor quality)

Skill Acquisition	My Rating	On-site Supervisor	School Job Coach	Comments
Begins work	2	2	2	
Follows directions from supervisor	3	2	2	Needs to be asked more than once
Asks for help when needed	1	1	1	Gets stuck when there is a problem
Quality of work	3	3	3	
Pace of work	2	2	2	
Interacts with coworkers	2	2	2	Needs some prompts
Other skill				

Figure 8.5. Daily job training data sheet.

The last data collection tool that Jenny decided to use was a rubric to measure listening skills since one of her students, Sharon, was having difficulty when communicating with coworkers on a job site. The job coach felt that this skill was critical to the student's success for future employment. The rubric had a scale of 1-4 for three different skills that contribute to good listening behavior. These skills could be rated each day the student was on the job site and total scores graphed and compared. An example of the completed basic communication skills rubric may be found in Figure 8.6. This rubric was completed weekly for Sharon by one of the paraprofessionals in Jenny's class.

Basic Communication Rubric: Listening Skills

Name: Sharon Kennedy	Date: 9/25/15
Activity: Hospital Laundry Job	Rater: Chloe Randall

Circle the appropriate indicator for each behavior.

Behavior	0	1	2	3	4	Points Received
Uses eye gaze appropriately	Does not look at person talking when prompted	Looks at person talking when prompted	Looks at person talking for brief moment	Looks at person talking for sustained period	Shifts gaze appropriately towards communication partner	3
Responds on topic	Does not respond	Responds on a different topic or responds on topic when prompted	Responds on topic 50% of the time	Responds on topic 75% of the time	Responds on topic 100% of the time	2
Waits his or her turn to talk/doesn't interrupt	Does not wait for his/her turn; Interrupts	Needs prompt or cue to wait for his/her turn; Does not interrupt	Waits his or her turn to talk 50% of the time	Waits his or her turn to talk 75% of the time	Waits his or her turn to talk 100% of the time	1

0	1	2	3	4
No success, even with help	Partial success at the 2.0 or 3.0 level with help	Independent success at 2.0 level	Independent success at 3.0 level	Independent success with more complex skill

Based on Marzano, R. J. (2010). *Formative assessment and standards-based grading.* Bloomington, IN: Marzano Resarch Laboratory.

Figure 8.6 Basic communication rubric.

These three teachers each taught in different environments and had different data collection needs. The solutions they selected are just some of the options that teachers have available as they try to "tame the data monster." Using the information in this book, you will be able to select your own data collection forms, procedures for collecting and analyzing the data, and organize your data collection procedures to have the same type of success our teachers had.

Chapter 9
Frequently Asked Questions

1. I'm too busy with students. How do I take data without it interfering with my teaching?

The key to taking data in a way that does not interfere with teaching is to integrate the process into your instruction. Of course, if you are working with one student or one student within a small group at a time, it is much easier to do. If you are recording event-by-event data, data recording should occur at the end of each trial during the interval. You can allow the student to engage with a reinforcing item or activity while you record the data. When you are working with a small group of students at one time, you need to organize your teaching so that there are natural pauses — you can either allow students to engage in a reinforcing item or activity for a short period of time or give them independent seat work to complete while you record the data. If you are leading a whole-class activity, train a paraprofessional to take the data and organize the data collection by student and day(s) of the week.

2. There are so many data sheets to choose from. How do I decide which one to use?

Select data sheets that are comfortable for you. Sometimes it is necessary to try several data collection systems to find one that works for you and for the other staff members who are taking data in your classroom. The data sheet must fit the skill or behavior you are tracking. Several data collection sheets in this book are useful for skill acquisition and others for functional assessment of behavior and tracking behavior targeted in IEP goals and objectives or behavior intervention plans. Some of the data sheets are useful when you are working in a 1:1 setting, whereas others allow you to take data on multiple students simultaneously. Choose the ones that fit into your classroom instructional design and that you find efficient.

3. I would like to have my aides take data when they are with the students. How can I make them understand that it is important for them to do this?

In order for all of the classroom staff to be comfortable taking data, several elements must be put into place. First, the aides must be trained to take data and be coached during the process to ensure that they are taking data correctly. Second, the data collection must be included in the zoning plan so that each member of the classroom team knows when he or she is responsible for data collection and for what students. Third, all of the classroom staff must take part in a regularly scheduled data review so that they see that the data they are taking are used to inform instruction and that data collection is an important part of each student's educational program.

4. I take lots of data, but I have difficulty finding the time to go back and review the information. What do you suggest?

Collecting data is a good first step to meet the requirements for student accountability and reporting progress to parents. However, it is the rare classroom teacher who uses the data to inform daily instruction. The self-graphing data sheets in this book are helpful because they do not require an extra step to get the data organized for review. When data is taken on other data sheets, it is often necessary to either graph it by hand or enter it into an Excel spreadsheet that can summarize the data in graph form. It is helpful to set aside time one day a week for data analysis and review so that the data sheets for the next week can be adjusted to reflect changes to steps in a teaching program or instructional targets themselves. In their work at the Baudhuin Preschool of Nova Southeastern University, the authors collaborated with the staff to establish Thursday afternoons for all classrooms after the students are dismissed to enter and analyze data in order to prepare new data sheets for the next week. No other meetings or activities are scheduled for that time.

5. I just grab any writing implement I can find to take data with. Does it matter what type of writing instrument I use?

It is important to record data in pen. First of all, it is more durable than pencil. Second, if the data must be photocopied, it is easier to read the data collected on the copy. Third, if the data is used in a due process case, it eliminates accusations of possibly erasing and changing the data.

6. I try to protect the identity of my students when taking data, so I only put their initials on the data sheet. Is that a problem?

While it is admirable that you want to protect the identity of your students, if a data sheet were to make its way out of your classroom, it is critical that there is no question about to whom the data belongs. The student's full name should always be placed on each data sheet so that if the data needs to be located and reviewed later on, it is clear who it belongs to. It is also important that the full date be put on the data sheet so that it is clear what year the data was collected. This is especially true for students in self-contained special education classrooms who may have the same teacher for multiple years. Placing a cover with construction paper over the data sheets on the clipboard will help preserve confidentiality when full names appear on the sheets.

7. In addition to IEP goals, I have trouble deciding what else I should be taking data on. What should I think about in deciding that?

IEP goals/objectives represent a relatively small number of skills and behaviors that are addressed in the classroom. For students who are in general education settings, the weekly spelling tests and end-of-unit tests represent a measure of mastery of a broad range of curricular content. Special education teachers don't usually have those types of measures available to them. The curriculum-based assessments included with alternate curricula like the ULS (https://www.n2y.com/products/unique) and STAR (Arick et al., 2004) provide measures of a broader range of skills, but may not be taken often enough. If certain curricular skills represent a particular area of need for a student that is not included in the IEP, you may want to track those skills. For example, for a student who has an IEP goal in math that focuses on money and measurement, it may still be important to track progress on an important skill like identifying key words in math word problems.

8. Summarizing the data is often an extra step. How can I set up a system that avoids that?

As much as possible, use a self-graphing data sheet or summarize the data as you go along. We have provided you with a variety of data sheets that summarize or make it easier for you to visually inspect the trend in the data, but it is important to keep looking for tools that make your job easier. Some of the applications that are available for iPads and smartphones allow you to send the data to your email account and summarize it for you.

9. How many data points do I have to have in order to make an informed decision about whether the student is making progress?

Farlow and Snell (1994) propose that you need at least five data points on a skill or behavior to assess progress; three of them should be current. That assumes that the student is not having a problem. If the student is not making progress in a smooth manner, they suggest that you need at least six data points to determine the data's trend.

10. How much data do I need to take each day?

The amount of data you collect depends upon the needs of your students. When you have a student or students who are making steady progress, you need fewer data points. When you have students whose progress is irregular, you need more data points in order to problem solve the instructional situation. We generally ask teachers to take data samples of five data points per week for a particular objective on the IEP when the instruction is embedded into daily classroom activities like art, morning meeting, or story time. When the objective is addressed in small-group teacher instruction, we ask the teacher to take daily data. During the time a student is in the independent work area completing a series of already mastered tasks and the objective is to build independence, we ask the teachers to take data once a week, which gives them approximately nine data points during the marking period to use to report progress.

11. I get overwhelmed thinking about data. How should I start the process?

To avoid feeling overwhelmed at the idea of data collection and analysis, approach the task as you approach teaching your students a complex skill: Break down data collection into manageable pieces. It is often easiest to start data collection with something that does not make you anxious and does not require you to do something that is not part of your usual routine. The labels that we described in Chapter 3 are easy to fill out and attach to work product that the students are completing anyway. This gives you the opportunity to evaluate the amount of assistance needed and the accuracy with which the student performs work that is done as part of the typical day. Another tip is to choose a time when you are working individually with a student or with a dyad of students, where you can take data on one student at a time and record that. You can alternate the days you take data on each member of the dyad two to three days per week. Slowly add students and/or activities in a way that does not challenge you.

References

Access points. Retrieved from http://www.cpalms.org/Public/search/AccessPoint#0

Arick, J. R., Loos, L., Falco, R., & Krug, D. A. (2004). *Strategies for teaching based on autism research.* Austin, TX: ProEd.

Behavior Tracker Pro. Retrieved from behaviortrackerpro.com

Brigance Compehensive Inventory for Basic Skills-II. (2010). North Billerica, MA: Curriculum Associates.

Browder, D., Liberty, K., Heller, M., & D'Huyvetterf, K. K. (1986). Self-management by teachers: Improving instructional decision making. *Professional School Psychology, 1*(3), 165-175.

Browder, D. M., & Spooner, F. (2011). *Teaching students with moderate and severe disabilities.* New York, NY: Guilford Press.

Buron, K. D., & Curtis, M. (2012). *The incredible 5-point scale: The significantly improved and expanded second edition; Assisting students in understanding social interactions and controlling their emotional responses.* Shawnee Mission, KS: AAPC Publishing.

Cooper, J. O., Heron, T. E., & Heward, W. L. (2007). *Applied behavior analysis* (2nd ed.). Upper Saddle River, NJ: Pearson Prentice Hall.

Cummings, A. R., & Carr, J. E. (2009). Evaluating progress in behavioral programs for children with autism spectrum disorders via continuous and discontinuous measurement. *Journal of Applied Behavior Analysis, 42*(1), 57-71.

D.A.T.A. Retrieved from behaviorscience.org

Durand, V. M., & Crimmons, D. B. (1988). Identifying the variables maintaining self-injurious behavior. *Journal of Autism and Developmental Disorders, 18,* 99-117.

Dunlap, G., Iovannone, R., Kincaid, D., Wilson, K., Christiansen, K., Strain, P., & English, C. (2010). *Prevent teach reinforce: The school-based model of individualized positive behavior support.* Baltimore, MD: Paul H. Brookes.

Farlow, L. J., & Snell, M. E. (1994). *Making the most of student performance data.* Washington, DC: American Association on Mental Retardation.

Fuchs, L. S., & Fuchs, D. (1986). Effects of systematic formative evaluation: A meta-analysis. *Exceptional Children, 53,* 199-208.

Haring, N., Liberty, K., & White, O. (1980). Rules for data-based strategy decisions in instructional programs: Current research and instructional implications. In W. Sailor, B. Wilcox, & L. Brown (Eds.), *Methods of instruction for severely handicapped students* (pp. 159-192). Baltimore, MD: Paul H. Brookes.

Henry, S. A., & Myles, B. S. (2013). *The comprehensive autism planning system (CAPS) for individuals with autism spectrum disorders and related disabilities: Integrating evidence-based practices throughout the student's day: Second edition.* Shawnee Mission, KS: AAPC Publishing.

Jimenez, B. A., Mims, P. J., & Browder, D. M. (2012). Data-based decisions guidelines for teachers of students with severe intellectual and developmental disabilities. *Education and Training in Autism and Developmental Disabilities, 47*(4), 407-413.

Kabot, S. S., & Reeve, C. E. (2014). Curriculum and class structure. In L. Wilkinson (Ed.), *Autism spectrum disorders in children and adolescents: Evidence-based assessment and intervention in schools. APA division 16 (school psychology) book series.* Washington, DC: American Psychological Association Press.

Lerman, D. C., Dittinger, L. H., Fentress, G., & Lanagan, T. (2011). A comparison of methods for collecting data on performance during discrete trial teaching. *Behavior Analysis in Practice, 4*(1), 53-62.

Links. Retrieved from http://linkscurriculum.com

Marzano, R. J. (2010). *Formative assessment & standards-based grading.* Bloomington, IN: Marzano Research Laboratory.

Partington, J. W. (2006). *The assessment of basic language and learning skills – Revised.* Pleasant Hill, CA: Behavior Analysts, Inc.

Reeve, C. E., & Carr, E. G. (2000). Prevention of severe behavior problems in children with developmental disabilities. *Journal of Positive Behavior Interventions, 2,* 144-160.

Reeve, C. E., & Kabot, S. S. (2012). *Building independence: How to create and use structured work systems.* Shawnee Mission, KS: AAPC Publishing.

Riffel, L. (n.d.). *The minute by minute duration data sheet.* Retrieved from www.behaviordoctor.org

Sandall, S. R., Schwartz, I. S., & LaCroix, B. (2004). Interventionists' perspectives about data collection in integrated early childhood classrooms. *Journal of Early Intervention, 26*(3), 161-174.

Sundberg, M. L. (2008). VB-MAPP *Verbal behavior milestones assessment and placement program.* Concord, CA: AVB Press.

Super Duper Data Tracker. Retrieved from http://www.superduperinc.com/products/view.aspx?stid=631#.VPy-dxIHF_UQ

Unique Learning System. Retrieved from https://www.n2y.com/products/unique

Wolery, M., Bailey Jr., D. B., & Sugai, G. M. (1988). Effective teaching: *Principles and procedures of applied behavior analysis with exceptional students.* Boston, MA: Allyn and Bacon, Inc.

Glossary

Aim Line. A line drawn on a graph from the level of a skill at the beginning of instruction and extending over the course of instruction to the target expected to be reached at the end of the grading period or school year (Farlow & Snell, 1984). An aim line is projected beyond the data collected so that you can compare the student's progress to see if it is following the line to mastery.

Antecedent. The environmental condition that is in existence when the behavior that is of interest occurs.

Applied Behavior Analysis (ABA). The science that improves socially significant behavior using the principles of behavior analysis and identifies the variables that cause the improvement in behavior using experimental procedures (Cooper et al., 2007).

Behavior. The activity of living organisms (Cooper et al., 2007).

Behavior Support Program. Interventions that are provided that reduce the likelihood that challenging behaviors will occur. These interventions may include preventive strategies, replacement behaviors, and responsive strategies.

Benchmarks. Steps along the way to meeting an IEP goal (e.g., attend 10 minutes, 20 minutes, 30 minutes).

Comprehensive Autism Programming System-Teaching Plan (CAPS-TP). A modification to the Comprehensive Autism Planning System that begins with the goal/objective or skill and operationalizes how that skill will be taught and generalized and how progress will be documented (Kabot & Reeve, 2014).

Chaining. A procedure for teaching sequences of steps of a skill to make up a more complex behavior.

Consequence. Environmental events that occur following the exhibition of a behavior.

Data Analysis. Review of a dimension of a skill or behavior to determine patterns of results.

Data Collection. Information that is gathered to measure a dimension of a skill or behavior.

Discrete Trial Training (DTT). An instructional strategy based on the operant conditioning paradigm that contains five steps: Provide a discriminative stimulus or direction, Prompt the student if necessary, The student response, The consequence or reinforcement the student earns, and the intertrial interval that shows the clear end of the trial and the clear onset of the next discrete trial (Cooper et al., 2007).

Duration. The length of time a behavior lasts.

Event Recording. A measure of the number of times a behavior occurs.

Frequency Recording. A count of the number of times a skill is performed or behavior occurs.

Functional Analysis. An assessment process in which experimental conditions are set up in a person's environment to manipulate the conditions under which functions of behavior can be identified by presenting four conditions separately: contingent attention, contingent escape, alone, and a high reinforcement condition where the behavior is not expected to occur.

Functional Behavior Assessment. An assessment method for obtaining information about the reasons (functions) a challenging behavior occurs.

Functional Routine. A task analysis of the steps or components of a routine that occur in the same manner with high frequency (e.g., toileting, morning meeting, eating in the cafeteria; Arick et al., 2004).

Goal. An annual, measureable outcome expected to be met within 1 year's time on an IEP or IHP. On IFSPs, goals are written for 6 months' duration.

Individual Education Program (IEP). Students who are eligible for special education under the Individuals with Disabilities Education Act have an IEP developed by the team that includes a clear description of the student's present level of performance, goals and objectives to work on for the next year, and the services and supports needed to accomplish those goals and objectives.

Individual Family Support Plan (IFSP). Children, birth to age 3 years, with developmental delays or established conditions, receive services under Part C of the Individuals with Disabilities Education Act through goals and objectives written in an IFSP.

Individual Habilitation Plan (IHP). Adults who are receiving services through Medicaid Waiver or Intermediate Care Facility funds have a plan that includes goals and objectives written to guide the habilitation program received and addresses recreation, vocational, residential, activities of daily living, and behavior.

Intensity/Severity. The magnitude of the behavior often measured by amount of property destruction or injury to persons.

Interval Data. Measurement that is taken by dividing an observation into set periods of time and recording the presence or absence for part or all of that period (Cooper et al., 2007).

Latency Data. Measurement of the amount of time that passes between when a direction is given and the person starts performing the behavior (Cooper et al., 2007).

Mastery. The criteria that are set to determine whether the individual has learned a skill to a level that he can use it in untrained situations.

Momentary Interval Data Collection. Measurement of a behavior in which the behavior is counted as occurring if it is observed either at the beginning or the end of the set period of time (Cooper et al., 2007).

Naturalistic instruction. Teaching that is embedded within common routines and contexts.

Objectives. Subskills that lead to mastery of an annual goal.

Partial Interval Data Collection. Measurement of a behavior where the behavior is counted as occurring if it happens at any time during the set period of time (Cooper et al., 2007).

Pivotal Response Training (PRT). Sometimes referred to as massed incidental teaching (Arick et al., 2004), PRT is based on the premise that teaching specific pivotal skills leads to faster acquisition of skills. It is a naturalistic form of instruction that is often used for teaching play, social interaction, and expressive communication skills.

Quantitative Data. Measurement of a dimension of skill or behavior that is numerical in nature.

Qualitative Data. Description of a dimension of skill or behavior that is non-numerical in nature.

Rate. A ratio of count or frequency per time (e.g., 3 hits per hour).

Rating Scale. A scale with defined points along a continuum that assigns a quantitative or qualitative value to an observed behavior.

Rubric. A set of criteria to rate student behavior or work that quantifies the qualitative nature of work consistently.

Sample Data. Collection of data for specified periods of time to gain an estimate that can be generalized to a larger time period. For instance, taking data in a 15-minute interval 4 times per day to gain an estimate of the frequency of humming across the day. When taking a sample of data, consistent procedures must be followed in order to get valid information about the occurrence of behavior.

Scatterplot. A data collection process that creates a picture or diagram showing the relationship between individual measures of a behavior with respect to the descriptors on the X and Y axis (Cooper et al., 2007).

Skill Acquisition. Teaching procedures that are designed to help an individual learn a new skill (e.g., discrete trial teaching, task analysis).

Structured Work Systems. An intervention developed by Project TEACCH at the University of North Carolina to visually structure and organize several tasks that a person has previously mastered to allow independent completion of multiple tasks in a series (Reeve & Kabot, 2012).

Task Analysis. A teaching procedure in which a complex skill is broken down into component steps (Cooper et al., 2007).

Time Sampling. A measure of whether a behavior occurs or not within a set interval of time (Cooper et al., 2007).

Trend Line. A line depicting the direction and rate of change in data that has already been collected. Typically created from a statistical regression, it can be computed in several ways based on data collected to determine if the student's progress is moving in the right direction. For instance, you would use a trend line to predict if a learner's behavior is decreasing after implementation of a behavior support plan.

Whole Interval Data Collection. An interval measure for behavior in which the behavior is counted as occurring if it is observed over the entire set period of time (Cooper et al., 2007).

Work Product / Permanent Product. A concrete sample or item resulting from a student's work, such as a completed worksheet or a picture of a job completed.

Zoning Plan. A schedule of the day that outlines each staff member's responsibilities for assigned students, activity areas of the classroom, lesson implementation, data collection, and other tasks that must be completed (Kabot & Reeve, 2014).

Appendix A
Directions for Completing Data Sheets

Discrete Trial Data Collection Form

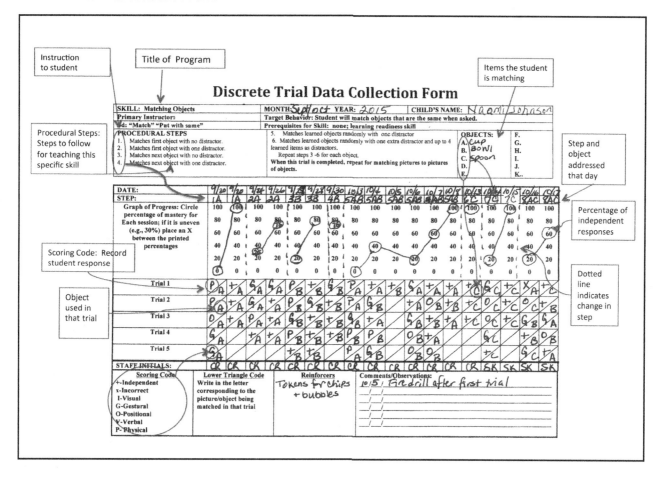

This form allows you to take data on specific skills in a discrete trial format and graph the data each day as it is taken, thus saving the time it would take to do this later. A significant amount of information is included on the sheet, so we felt that it would be helpful to provide directions on how to complete it. You can also find a video on how to use the data sheet at https://www.aapcpublishing.net/bookstore/books/9123.aspx.

First, you will need to fill in the information at the top of the form that provides details about the program and the student. When preparing to work with the specific student, write the student's name and the year data will be collected. Writing the year allows you to assure that you will still be able to go back years later and know when the data was collected.

The Target Behavior defines the program objective, in this case, matching common objects. *Prerequisite Skills* are the skills that the student needs to have learned before you begin to teach this specific skill. *Objects, or Targets,* are the items specifically being taught in each trial (e.g., objects to be matched). Listing them allows everyone working with the learner to know what item to target as well as to record that information by the letter code in the data to review later.

After you have identified the target skill, the steps to reach the goal (i.e., the task analysis) are written under *Procedural Steps*. These steps are numbered to allow for easy recording while taking data. The SD is the cue or instruction that tells the student what to do (e.g., saying "sit down" for teaching 1-step commands). This ensures some level of consistency among instructors about the words that are used to present the skill. Finally, the *Primary Instructor* is the instructor who works with the student most frequently; it may include more than one person.

Each column represents a session or part of a session of discrete trials for a specific student. Mark the date for each session of trials in the row labeled "date" at the top of the column in which data will be collected during a given session.

Underneath the date, record data for each *Trial* presented. Students may complete five trials or opportunities per day within one setting or across settings. If they have more than five trials, you can move to the next column. For each trial, in the upper-left-hand corner, record the level of assistance the student required to complete the step on the trial according to the *Scoring Code* at the bottom of the page. In the lower triangle of the box for each trial, record the object (or target) that was the focus of the trial (e.g., A for cup). This will allow you to assess if some targets are mastered while others are not when you present multiple objects in a randomized fashion.

At the bottom of the page, next to the scoring code, is a box for writing in the learner's reinforcers. List the items that are commonly used to reinforce correct responses (e.g., tokens, candy, high five). Having this information in writing provides consistency across instructors. In the bottom right corner is a box for comments and notes. The date may be written on the left and the comment to the right of the date. In the example above, the instructor wrote that trials were stopped one day because of a fire drill that interrupted the session. This information can be helpful when going back to review the data.

The numbers to 100 represent a *Graph of Progress*. When five opportunities are recorded, put an X over or between the number(s) representing the percentage of mastery (e.g., 2 correct responses out of 5 would be 40%). Connect the Xs to draw a graph of progress. Do not connect Xs when steps change. Instead, when a step is mastered, draw a dashed line after the column in which the step was mastered to separate it from the next session when a new step is begun. This makes it easy to see when the instructor can move on to the next step and when the full program is mastered.

Other AAPC Books
by Christine Reeve and Susan Kabot ...

Setting up Classroom Spaces That Support Students With Autism Spectrum Disorders; foreword by Juane Heflin, PhD

Building Independence: How to Use Structured Work Systems; foreword by Gary Mesibov, PhD

To order, visit www.aapcpublishing.net

Advance Praise ...

"*Taming the Data Monster* is beneficial to any instructor whether in special or general education. It provides detailed instructions for setting up and maintaining accurate data collection in various settings, as well as how to analyze the data to make informed decisions regarding next steps. After reading this book, I am eager to revamp how I approach data collection in my classroom, and I feel very confident about 'taming' the monster that haunts me school year after school year. I cannot wait to share this book with the staff at my school!"

    – Gabrielle Dixon, teacher-blogger

"This book is truly amazing, a must-have for any educator! I've always taken data in the classroom but rarely felt it was productive. This book provides so many examples and realistic ways to both take and interpret data that the task becomes more doable. I'm actually excited to take data now!"

    – Brie Holtrop, high school special educator

11209 Strang Line Rd
Lenexa, KS 66215
www.aapcpublishing.net

CPSIA information can be obtained
at www.ICGtesting.com
Printed in the USA
BVOW03s0840030617

485621BV00008B/52/P

9 781942 197072